AF560145

SILKWORM HYBRIDS FOR TROPICS

SILKWORM HYBRIDS FOR TROPICS

By

Dr. K. Nagalakshmamma

M.Sc,(Ag). P.G.D.S

Associate Professor

Deptt. of Sericulture

Sri Padmavati Women's University

Tirupati – 517 502

Andhra Pradesh

(India)

DISCOVERY PUBLISHING HOUSE PVT. LTD.

NEW DELHI-110 002

Published by:
Tilak Wasan
DISCOVERY PUBLISHING HOUSE PVT. LTD.
4831/24, Prahlad Street, Ansari Road
Darya Ganj, New Delhi-110002 (India)
Phone : +91-11-23279245, 43764432
Fax : +91-11-23253475
E-mail : parul.wasan@gmail.com
discoverypublishinghouse@gmail.com
web : www.discoverypublishinggroup.com

***First Edition:* 2011**
ISBN: 978-81-8356-919-4

Silkworm Hybrids for Tropics

Printed at:
Shree Balaji Art Press
Delhi

Dedication

In the name of Goddess

SRI PADMAVATHI DEVI Ammavaru ...

Dedicated to

My Husband

Mukku Sathyavanthudu

Advocate & Congress Leader

FOREWORD

Sericulture has received prominence to its commercial significance in trade. The silkworm *Bombyx mori.*L. has been grown for cocoon crop and silk production which in turn provide livelihood to rural poor, particularly women. Silk production and its quality is well-known to be dependent on the breed of the silkworm. Development of silkworm hybrids with reference to region specific and season specific is the need based research.

Rayalseema of Andhra Pradesh in particular is having semi-arid environmental conditions and hence there is an immense need to identify the new silkworm hybrids specific to this region for increased cocoon production and income. This book based on Dr. K. Nagalakshmamma experimental work, wherein she identified some promising commercial hybrids of silkworm suitable to Rayalaseema climatic conditions.

This book provides valuable information about the protocols to identify the promising silkworm hybrids for commercial exploitation. It will be very useful not only to the practising sericulturists but also to the students of sericutlure. I commend the effort put forth by its author viz., Dr. K. Nagalakshmamma in bringing out such a useful book.

With appreciations and best wishes...

19/7/10

Dr. P. NAGESHAM
Asstt. Director of Sericulture
Tirupati

PREFACE

Andhra Pradesh is one of the leading producers of mulberry silk in India next only to Karnataka. Rayalaseema, the southern part of Andhra Pradesh which is one of the dry belts of the State bordering northern part of Karnataka is contributing the major share of silk produced in the State. The sericulture activity in the area is greatly influenced by the growth and development of sericulture in Karnataka as well as the geographic continuity and overlapping culture of two States. Most of the farmers with small holdings have taken up intensive cultivation of mulberry with assured irrigation facilities and engaged in commercial cocoon production by rearing multi-bivoltine hybrid, PM × NB_4D_2.

Even though, the multi bivoltine hybrids performed well, the unit production and the quality of the silk produced remains poor, since the inherent defects of Pure Mysore are passed on the hybrids. Therefore, the want of suitable productive and robust races to sustain the macro and micro environmental conditions appear to be one of the major constraints to the growth and development of sericulture in Rayalaseema region.

The science of breeding is aimed at providing optimal genotypes for the available environments. Even though incessant efforts have been made by silkworm breeders to synthesize highly productive races elsewhere in the country, it is rather unfortunate that such efforts have not been made to breed suitable races for Rayalaseema region. In view of the above, it is of paramount importance that the genotype of the available silkworm races in the country need to be studied intensively in order to reorganize the genotypes and synthesize the silkworm breeds responding favourable to the conditions prevailing in Rayalaseema region.

The suitability of a race/a hybrid not only depends on the genetic content but also on its ability to respond to different environmental conditions. In view of this, it is necessary to understand the stability in the performance of the race with regard to the expression of economic traits. It is clearly known that the seasonal differences in the environment considerably influence the phenotypic expression as well as the coefficient values of the heritability of the important characters such as cocoon weight, shell weight, cocoon shell ratio. In addition, the genetic balance as well the environment and other considerations would also affect the phenotypic expression. Realizing the importance of environmental conditions, several breeds have been developed by Japanese as well as Indian breeders suitable to different environmental conditions; however such attempts have not been made to synthesize the silkworm breeds suitable to the environmental conditions prevailing in Rayalaseema region.

In view of this, an attempt was made to develop suitable hybrid combinations for commercial exploitation in Rayalaseema region as a first step, a few multivoltine and bivoltine races developed in India were chosen to evaluate their performance in different seasons in Rayalaseema region in order to use them in different conditions to identify the promising hybrids. The performance of the three new multivoltine races MU_1, MU_{11}, MU_{303} and three new bivoltine races MU_{852}, MG_{414}, MG_{408} procured from the germplasm bank maintained in the University of Mysore was evaluated by rearing them in different seasons of the year along with their respective controls, PM and NB_4D_2. They were evaluated on the basis of eleven metric traits such as fecundity, hatching percentage, larval duration, larval weight, cocoon yield by number, cocoon yield by weight, cocoon weight, shall weight, shell ratio, filament length and rupation rate, studied in three different seasons.

The above races along with respective control PM and NB_4D_2 were utilized to understand the degree of heterosis, over dominance, general and specific combining ability, as well as the magnitude of the heterosis and over dominance expressed in the hybrids.

On the basis of the mean performance of the new hybrids, general combining ability of the parental races, specific combining ability as well the heterosis and over dominance of the hybrids, four hybrids viz., $MU_1 \times MU_{852}$, $MU_1 \times MG_{414}$, $MU_{11} \times MU_{852}$ and $MU_{303} \times MU_{852}$ were identified as superior to other hybrids and the control.

The evaluation of the new multi bihybrids under the field conditions prevailing in Rayalaseema also clearly pointed out the superiority of the new hybrids in their stability in the expression of economic characters. The versatility of the new hybrid is also reflected in the significant improvement of the cocoon yield as well the rate fetched per kg. of cocoons thus exhibiting improvement in both the quantity and the quality. These two parameters have substantially contributed to the significant improvement of 27.85% to 34.25% over the control. The improvement in the productivity, quality and profitability observed in the study certainly qualify the new multi × bi hybrids for commercial exploitation in Rayalaseema region making sericulture a more profitable venture enabling the industry for its all round growth and development.

In view of this they are adjudicated as the most promising multi × bivoltine hybrids suitable for commercial exploitation in the Rayalaseema region of Andhra Pradesh.

Author

ACKNOWLEDGEMENTS

I have great pleasure in expressing my deep sense of respect, sincere gratitude and whole hearted thanks to Dr. G. Sreerama Reddy, Professor of Sericulture (Retd), former UGC Emeritus Fellow, Department of Studies in Sericultural Sciences, University of Mysore, Manasagangothri, Mysore for his superrogated guidance, valuable suggestions, constructive criticism, inspiring encouragement and interest throughout this study.

I am thankful to Dr. P. Murali Mohan, Professor and Head, Department of Sericulture, Sri Padmavathi Mahila Viswavidyalayam, Tirupati for his encouragement and for providing facilities.

I acknowledge my thanks to my collegues Dr. D. Bharathi, Dr. P. Sujathamma, Dr. G. Savithri and non-teaching staff members Miss. Madhavi, Mrs. Durgadevi and Mrs. Shakeela for their encouragement and co-operation. I extend very warm thanks to Sri Chenchaiah, Sri Shankar, Sri Chiranjeevi, Smt. Bharathi and others for their kind help in laboratory work.

I owe my sincere thanks to the Assistant Director. Department of Sericulture. Government of Andhra Pradesh, Tirupati and his Staff as well the farmers for their co-operation in conducting the field study.

It is my privilege to express my sincere thanks to Dr. G.V. Kalpana. S.R.O., Dr. Nirmal Kumar, Deputy Director, CSR & TI, Mysore and Dr. L. Nanjundaswamy, Department of Studies in Sericulture Science. University of Mysore, Mysore, for their timely suggestions and wholehearted support.

I am highly grateful to Dr. Rekha Ballal, S.R.A., CSR & TI, Mysore for her helping hand in analyzing the data.

I gratefully remember my husband, Sri. Mukku Sathyavanthudu for his moral support, inspiration, encouragement and interest for the completion of this book.

My special thanks are due to my mother, K. Sivamma, mother-in-law, M. Kanthamma, Brothers K.V.S.Sudharsan and K.V.S. Jaganmohan, Sister-in-laws P. Sreelatha and B. Padmavathi and my beloved sister Dr. K. Radha and her husband U. Mohan and my children Mukku Lalasa, Mukku Samykya. Mukku Thulasi Kumar and Manjula, for their whole hearted support and inspiration throughout the study.

I specially place on to record deep sense of gratitude to Smt. Lakshmamma, Smt. P. Jayamma, G.S. Prakash and S. Shailaja Reddy, for their affectionate hospitality, encouragement and support during my stay at Mysore.

I acknowledge my profound thanks to Sri Sudhakar and his team, Maruthi Computer Centre, Gangothri Layout, Mysore for neat typing of the manuscript of the book.

I am deeply indebted for all those who continuously encouraged directly or indirectly to enable me to carry out this work successfully.

K. NAGALAKSHMAMMA

CONTENTS

CONTENTS

Chapter 1

SEASONAL STUDIES ON THE PERFORMANCE OF NEW MULTIVOLTINE AND BIVOLTINE RACES

INTRODUCTION

A clear understanding of genetic architecture and its variable response in the expression of economic traits of the silkworm races is an important step in order to utilize them as potential parents in the hybridization programme. The expression of economic traits in silkworm vary a great deal and influenced by the environmental factors to which they are exposed during growth and development. Therefore, the evaluation of the performance of the silkworm race is of vital importance to select the suitable parental material for hybridization programme. Further, recognizing the existence of favourable gene combinations during the course of the study also play an important role in achieving the desired objective of developing suitable hybrid combinations for commercial exploitation. The choice of the parental material largely helps to satisfy the requirement of the environmental conditions prevailing in a particular area in which they are commercially exploited.

Unlike, the temperate regions, where sericultural practices are confined to favourable seasons, the sericultural practices are seen through out the year in tropical climates as seen in India. Since the environmental conditions varied a great deal in tropical climates, manipulation of the temperature and relative humidity play a vital role in the successful harvest of the cocoon crops. Besides this, the genetic potential of the silkworm races in question is also of atmost importance. Therefore, the science of breeding is aimed at providing optimal genotypes for the available environments. The suitability of a race/a hybrid not only depends on the genetic content but also on its ability to respond to different environmental conditions. In view of this, it is necessary to understand the stability in the performance of the race with regard to the expression of economic traits (Raman and Ahmad, 1988). It is clearly known that the seasonal differences in the environment considerably influence the phenotypic expression as well as the coefficient values of the heritability of the important characters such as cocoon weight, shell weight, cocoon shell ratio (Nacheva and Zunka, 1989). In addition, the genetic balance as well the environmental and other considerations would also affect the phenotypic expression (Hirobe, 1956). Realizing the importance of environmental conditions, several breeds have been developed by Japanese as well as Indian breeders suitable to different environmental conditions. However such attempts have not been made to synthesize the silkworm breeds suitable to the environmental conditions prevailing in Rayalaseema region.

In view of this, an attempt is made to develop suitable hybrid combinations for commercial exploitation in Rayalaseema region. As a first step a few multivoltine and bivolitine races developed in India were chosen to evaluate their performance in different seasons in Rayalaseema region in order to use them in different combinations to identify the promising hybrids.

MATERIAL AND METHODS

The three new multivoltive races, MU_1, MU_{11}, MU_{303} and three new bivoltine races, MU_{852}, MG_{414}, MG_{408} developed in the Department of Studies in Sericultural Science, University of Mysore, Manasagangothri, Mysore, Karantaka and one multivoltine race, Pure Mysore (PM) and another bivoltine race, NB_4D_2 which are the parents of the ruling multibihybrid, PM × NB_4D_2 as controls were chosen for the study. The photographs of the cocoons of the new multivoltine and bivoltine races along with their respective control are depicted in Plates 1.1 and 1.2.

Basic stocks of the above races were procured from the germplasm bank, Department of Studies in Sericultural Science, University of Mysore, Manasagangothri, Mysore, Karantaka and were maintained in the Department of Sericulture, Sri Padmavathi Mahila Viswavidyalayam, Tirupathi, Andhra Pradesh by following standard methods of race maintenance.

Tirupathi enjoys both south-west monsoon from June to August and North-East monsoon from September to November. The rainfall is rather erratic and the climate is hot and dry during most part of the year. During June to November when monsoon is active, the period is designated as monsoon period which enjoys moderate temperature of 25-33°C, rainfall of 29-33cm and relative humidity of 30-75 per cent. The months from December to February rather exhibit moderate temperature of 15-33°C with low humidity of 30-60 per cent and rainfall of 3-30 cm, occasionally exhibiting short spells of heavy rainfall is designed as post-monsoon. On the other hand pre-monsoon which falls in the months of March and May is characterized by high temperature ranging from 30-40° C with a low relative humidity of 30-40 per cent with occasional showers at the end of May.

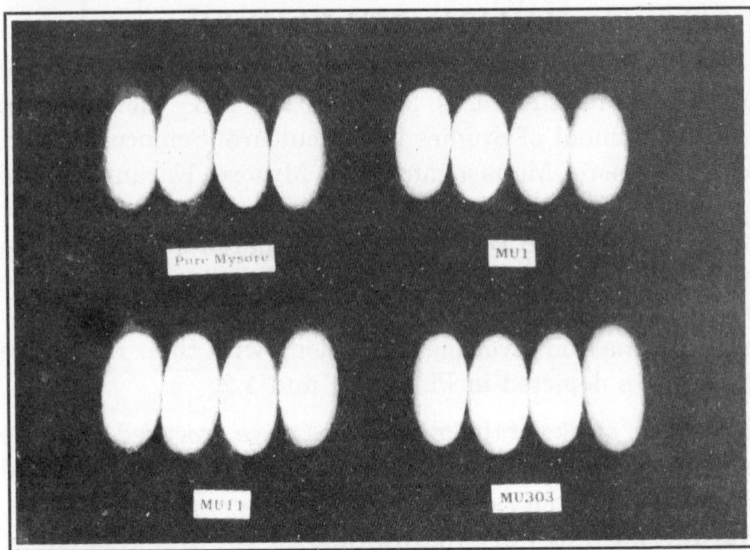

Plate – 1.1: Photograph of the Cocoons of Multivoltine Races and Pure Mysore

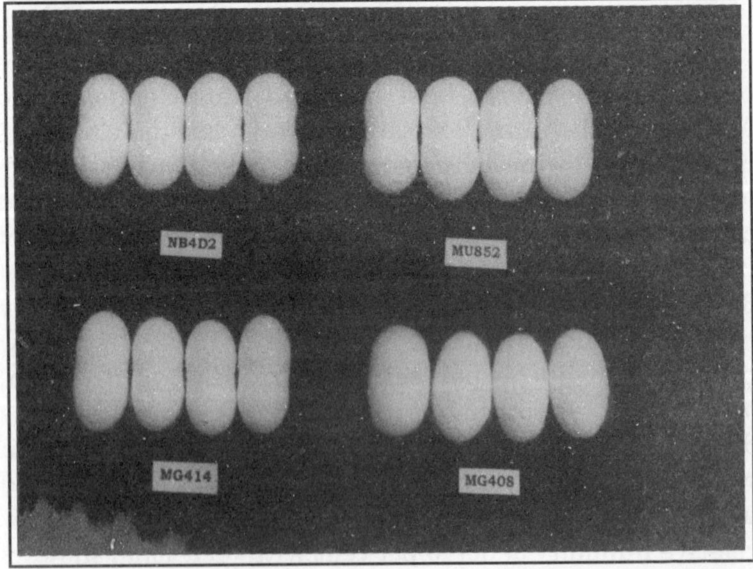

Plate – 1.2: Photograph of the Cocoons of Bivoltine Races and NB_4D_2

The experimental rearing was initiated by selecting five disease-free layings of each one of the eight races in three replicates. The eggs were incubated and black boxed at the pinhead stage to ensure synchrony in the embryonic development and uniform hatching. On the tenth day, the larvae were brushed into the rearing trays and chawki reared by following standard chawki rearing techniques (Narasimhand arid Krishnaswami, 1972) by feeding the mulberry leaf of M_5 variety harvested from the irrigated mulberry garden maintained in Sri Padmavathi Mahila Viswavidyalayam, Tirupathi. After the third moult, the rearing was conducted by keeping 300 larvae for each replicate. The late age rearing was conducted by following standard rearing techniques suggested by Yokoyama (1963) and Narasimhanna and Krishnaswami (1972). In spite of the best efforts made to maintain the recommended temperature of 26-28°C and relative humidity of 80-90 per cent during chawki stage and 24-26°C and relative humidity of 70-80 per cent during late age, the rearing room temperature and relative humidity varied from 18-35°C and 35-75 per cent respectively. In view of the fluctuating environmental conditions prevailing in tropics, utmost care was taken, throughout the rearing period by providing optimum quantity of leaf to ensure healthy growth and development by silkworms. The spinning worms were mounted on bamboo montages and harvested on the 6th day of spinning. Of the total of four rearings conducted for the study, two rearings were made in monsoon, one rearing in post-monsoon and the other rearing in pre-monsoon. The data pertaining to eleven economic traits were recorded for each replication to assess the performance of each race. The observations recorded for two rearings in monsoon season were averaged replication-wise and the replication mean value is taken for monsoon period, while the mean rearing data was taken for each pre-monsoon and post-monsoon periods. The data generated is tabulated replication-wise separately for multivoltine and bivoltine races for three different seasons and subjected to statistical analysis.

Each one of the eleven economic traits considered and evaluated for the study are described below:

Fecundity

The number of eggs in the brood laid by an individual moth is referred as fecundity. This is an important trait and is directly associated with the fitness of individuals and of populations. The reproductive success is often expressed in terms of fecundity denoting the number of eggs in a brood. The average fecundity was determined by using five disease free layings randomly selected for each race.

Hatching Percentage

The trait represents the number of eggs hatched synchronously in it, is expressed in percentage by using the following formula:

$$\text{Hatching Percentage} = \frac{\text{Total number of hatched eggs}}{\text{Total number of eggs in a laying}} \times 100$$

Larval Duration

It is the period from the day of hatching to the time of onset of spinning. It is expressed in hours. The total larval duration is inclusive of both moulting period and eating period. Shorter larval duration is considered to be of economic importance as it minimizes the leaf consumption, labour and mortality due to diseases. Reduction in mean values for this trait observed in many hybrids is considered as an improvement over the parents, leading to the expression of negative combining ability, heterosis and over dominance.

Larval Weight

It is a mean weight of ten randomly selected fully grown larvae taken one day before the commencement of the spinning. It denotes the healthiness and robustness of the larvae. It is expressed in grams.

Cocoon Yield by Number

It represents the mean number of cocoons harvested out of the unit number of larvae retained after third moult and converted to the standard unit of 10,000 larvae brushed. It denotes viability and is calculated by using the formula given below by taking the standard unit of 10,000 larvae brushed.

$$\text{Cocoon yield by number} = \frac{\text{Number of Cocoons harvested}}{\text{Number of larvae retained after } 3^{rd} \text{ moult}} \times 10000$$

Cocoon Yield by Weight

It is the total weight of live cocoons in kilograms for unit number of larvae retained after third moult and converted to the standard unit of 10,000 larvae brushed. This is an important character as it is directly associated with the economics of cocoon production. It is calculated by using the formula given here under.

$$\text{Cocoon yield by weight} = \frac{\text{Total weight of the coccons harvested}}{\text{Total Number of cocoon harvested}} \times \text{Yield by number}$$

Single Cocoon Weight

The average cocoon weight based on 25 male and 25 female cocoons taken at random on the 6th day of spinning is considered as the single cocoon weight. It is expressed in grams.

Single Shell Weight

This trait represents the total quantity of silk in a cocoon. It is the average weight of 25 male and 25 female cocoon shells. The shells taken for weighing are from the cocoons which were used for recording single cocoon weight. It is expressed in grams.

Cocoon Shell Ratio

It denotes the percentage of silk available in a single cocoon. It is the ratio between the average weight of 25 male and 25 female cocoon shells and the weight of a similar number of respective cocoons. It is calculated by using the following formula (Harada, 1961).

$$\text{Shell ratio} = \frac{\text{Average cocoon shell weight}}{\text{Average cocoon weight}} \times 100$$

Filament length

It is the total length of non-breakable silk filament reeled from the cocoon and is represented in metres. The mean value of filament length is obtained by reeling ten cocoons, collected randomly from each replicate on an epprouvate. It is measured in metres.

Filament length = Circumference of the epprouvate × Total number of rotations

Pupation Rate

Pupation rate is expressed in percentage and is calculated by the number of live pupae recovered out of unit number of cocoons harvested from the unit number of larvae retained after third moult as per the formula which is given below:

$$\text{Population ratio} = \frac{\text{Number of live purpae recovered}}{\text{Unit number of cocoon harvested}} \times 100$$

Statistical Analysis

The replication mean values obtained for each trait and for each race was subjected to analysis of variance by employing a statistical model for two-way classification by Kempthrone (1952) to analyse the variation among the seasons, among the races and for the interaction effect between season and race. Kempthrone (1952) model reads as follows:

$$Y_{ij} = V + S_j + (RS)_{ij} - e_{ij}$$

Where,

Y_{ij} = Effect of ith race in j^{th} season

V = Constant effect

Sj = Effect of jth season

$(RS)_{ij}$ = Interaction effect of ith race in j^{th} season

e_{ij} = Random component effect

Results

The rearing data pertaining to eleven metric traits of the three new multivoltine races, MU_1, MU_{11} and MU_{303} and the three new bivoltine races, MU_{852}, MG_{414} and MG_{408} along with the respective controls Pure Mysore and NB_4D_2 recorded for three different seasons is assembled separately for each character, statistically analysed and presented in tables 1.1 to 1.11 for multivoltines and Table 1.12 to Table 1.22 for bivoltines.

MULTIVOLTINE RACES

Fecundity

Perusal of the data (*Table 1.1*) revealed that all the three new multivoltine races were found to record higher fecundity compared to the control, PM (394.44). Among the new races, the mean fecundity was observed to vary from 468.22 (MU_1) to 478.77 (MU_{11}). It was found to be higher in monsoon (465.00) followed by Post-monsoon (453.58) and pre-monsoon (445.75).

The analysis of variance revealed significant variability for fecundity ($P<0.05$) among races and seasons. The interaction between race and season was found to be non-significant.

Hatching Percentage

The results obtained for hatching percentage (*Table 1.2*) revealed that all the three new multivoltine races were found to excel that of the control, PM (87.98%).

Table 1.1: Mean Performance of Fecundity (number) in Multivoltine Races

Race (R)	Season (s)			
	Pre-monsoon	Monsoon	Post-monsoon	Mean
MU_1	456.66 (21.36)	481.33 (21.93)	466.66 (21.60)	468.22 (21.63)
MU_{11}	471.33 (21.71)	484.00 (22.00)	481.00 (21.93)	478.77 (21.88)
MU_{303}	471.33 (21.70)	488.00 (22.09)	473.66 (21.76)	477.66 (21.85)
PM	383.66 (19.58)	406.66 (20.16)	393.00 (19.82)	394.44 (19.86)
Mean	445.75 (21.11)	465.00 (21.56)	453.58 (21.28)	–

Note: Values in parentheses are angular transformed values.

ANOVA

Source of Variation	df	MSS	F ratio	CD at 5%
Replication	2	0.0176	0.43^{NS}	–
Season (S)	2	0.6289	15.63*	0.16
Race (R)	3	8.5023	211.41*	0.19
Interaction (S × R)	6	0.0225	0.55^{NS}	0.33
Error	22	0.0402		

* Significant.

NS: Non-significant.

The mean values for this trait was found to vary from 94.54% (MU_1) to 96.32% (MU_{11}) among the new races and was found to vary from 92.36% (pre-monsoon) to 94.93% (post-monsoon) among the seasons.

The analysis of variance revealed that the trait, hatching percentage was observed to vary significantly ($P < 0.05$) among the races and seasons and was observed to be non significant ($P > 0.05$) for the interaction between season and race.

Table 1.2: Mean Performance of Hatching Percentage in Multivolitne Race

Race (R)	Season (s)			Mean
	Pre-monsoon	Monsoon	Post-monsoon	
MU_1	93.36 (9.66)	94.46 (9.71)	95.80 (9.78)	94.54 (9.72)
MU_{11}	96.25 (9.81)	95.85 (9.79)	96.86 (9.84)	96.32 (9.81)
MU_{303}	94.16 (9.70)	95.24 (9.75)	95.60 (9.77)	95.00 (9.74)
PM	85.70 (9.25)	86.76 (9.31)	91.48 (9.56)	87.98 (9.37)
Mean	92.36 (9.61)	93.08 (9.64)	94.93 (9.74)	–

Note: Values in parentheses are angular transformed values.

ANOVA

Source of Variation	df	MSS	F ratio	CD at 5%
Replication	2	0.0031	0.54^{NS}	–
Season (S)	2	0.0577	10.34*	0.06
Race (R)	3	0.3420	61.27*	0.07
Interaction (S × R)	6	0.0136	2.43^{NS}	0.12
Error	22	0.0056		

* Significant.

NS: Non-significant.

Larval Duration

Perusal of the data given in Table 1.3 revealed that all the three new multivoltine races were found to register shorter larval duration compared to the control, PM (664.66 hrs). Among the new races the trait was found to vary from 554.66 hrs (MU_{11}) to 565.33 hrs (MU_{303}). The larval duration was observed to vary from 554.00 h (pre-monsoon) to 613.50 hrs (post-monsoon). The interaction between season and race

Table 1.3: Mean performance of Larval Duration (Hours) in Multivoltine Races

Race (R)	Season (s)			Mean
	Pre-monsoon	Monsoon	Post-monsoon	
MU_1	530.00 (23.02)	568.00 (23.83)	580.00 (24.08)	559.33 (23.65)
MU_{11}	522.00 (22.84)	558.00 (23.62)	584.00 (24.16)	554.66 (23.55)
MU_{303}	542.00 (23.28)	568.00 (23.83)	586.00 (24.20)	565.33 (23.77)
PM	622.00 (24.94)	668.00 (25.84)	704.00 (26.53)	664.66 (25.78)
Mean	554.00 (23.53)	590.50 (24.30)	613.50 (24.76)	–

Note: Values in parentheses are angular transformed values.

ANOVA

Source of variation	df	MSS	F ratio	CD at 5%
Replication	2	0.0117	1.18^{NS}	–
Season (S)	2	4.5898	465.76*	0.08
Race (R)	3	10.1699	1032.01*	0.09
Interaction (S × R)	6	0.0736	7.46*	0.16
Error	22	0.0099		

* Significant

NS: Non-significant

revealed that MU_{11} was found to record the shortest larval duration (522.00 h) in pre-monsoon compared to others.

The analysis of variance revealed that the trait, was found to vary significantly ($P<0.05$) among races and seasons and also for interaction between season and race.

Larval Weight

The data presented in Table 1.4 revealed that all the three new multivoltine races were found to record higher larval weight compared to the control, PM (26.70 g). The mean larval weight, among the new races was observed to vary from 33.34 g (MU_{303}) to 33.73 g (MU_1) and among the seasons from 30.52 g (pre-monsoon) to 33.14g (monsoon). The interaction between the season and race revealed that MU_{303} was found to record the highest value (35.50 g) compared to others in monsoon.

Table 1.4: Mean Performance of Larval Weight (Grams) in Multivoltine Races

Race (R)	Season (s)			Mean
	Pre-monsoon	Monsoon	Post-monsoon	
MU_1	32.61	34.32	34.28	33.73
MU_{11}	31.90	35.31	33.51	33.57
MU_{303}	32.23	35.50	32.30	33.34
PM	25.37	27.43	27.30	26.70
Mean	30.52	33.14	31.84	–

ANOVA

Source of variation	df	MSS	F ratio	CD at 5%
Replication	2	0.5605	0.93^{NS}	–
Season (S)	2	20.4629	34.04*	0.65
Race (R)	3	105.9388	176.26*	0.75
Interaction (S × R)	6	1.8639	3.10*	1.30
Error	22	0.6010		

* Significant.

NS: Non-significant.

The analysis of variance revealed that the trait was found to vary significantly ($P < 0.05$) among races, seasons and also for interaction between race and season.

Cocoon Yield by Number

The analysis of data given in Table 1.5 revealed that all the three new multivoltine races were found to record higher cocoon yield by number compared to the control, PM (8739.11). The mean values of the trait was observed to vary, among the new races from 9125.66 (MU_{303}) to 9214.32 (MU_1) and among the seasons from 8646.33 (pre-monsoon) to 9483.00 (monsoon).

Table 1.5: Mean performance of cocoon yield by number in multivoltine races

Race (R)	Season (s)			Mean
	Pre-monsoon	Monsoon	Post-monsoon	
MU_1	8899.66 (94.33)	9610.66 (98.03)	9132.66 (95.56)	9214.33 (95.99)
MU_{11}	8710.66 (93.33)	9677.66 (98.37)	9077.33 (95.27)	9155.22 (95.68)
MU_{303}	8644.00 (92.97)	9577.66 (97.86)	9155.33 (95.68)	9125.66 (95.52)
PM	8333.00 (91.28)	9066.00 (95.21)	8818.33 (93.90)	8739.11 (93.48)
Mean	8646.83 (92.98)	9483.00 (97.38)	9045.91 (95.11)	–

Note: Values in parentheses are angular transformed values.

ANOVA

Source of variation	df	MSS	F ratio	CD at 5%
Replication	2	0.0469	0.04^{NS}	–
Season (S)	2	57.8906	60.28*	0.82
Race (R)	3	11.7083	12.19*	0.95
Interaction (S × R)	6	0.7448	0.77^{NS}	1.65
Error	22	0.9602		

* Significant.

NS: Non-significant.

The analysis of variance revealed that cocoon yield by number was found to vary significantly ($P<0.05$) among races and seasons and the interaction between season and race was found to be non-significant ($P>0.05$).

Cocoon Yield by Weight

The results obtained for cocoon yield by weight (Table 1.6) revealed that all the three new multivoltine races were observed to record higher cocoon yield by weight compared to the control, PM (9.17 kgs). The mean values for this trait was noticed to vary among the races from 11.17 kgs (MU_{303}) to 11.26 kgs (MU_1) and among the seasons from 9.89 kgs (pre-monsoon) to 11.44 kgs (monsoon).

Table 1.6: Mean Performance of Cocoon Yield by Weight (Kilograms) in Multivoltine Races

Race (R)	Pre-monsoon	Season (s) Monsoon	Post-monsoon	Mean
MU_1	10.75	11.90	11.14	11.26
MU_{11}	10.48	11.90	11.13	11.17
MU_{000}	10.35	11.87	11.31	11.18
PM	8.01	10.10	9.42	9.17
Mean	9.89	11.44	10.75	–

ANOVA

Source of variation	df	MSS	F ratio	CD at 5%
Replication	2	0.0259	0.28^{NS}	–
Season (S)	2	7.2002	80.51*	0.25
Race (R)	3	9.2570	103.52*	0.29
Interaction (S × R)	6	0.1786	1.99^{NS}	0.50
Error	22	0.0894		

* Significant.

NS: Non-significant.

The analysis of variance revealed that the cocoon yield by weight was found to vary significantly ($P<0.05$) among races and seasons and was found to be non significant ($P > 0.05$) for the interaction between season and race.

Cocoon Weight

Perusal of the data revealed that all the three new multivoltine races were found to record higher cocoon weight compared to the control, PM (1.05 g) (Table 1.7). The mean cocoon weight was observed to vary among the new races from 1.22 g (MU_{11}) to 1.22 g (MU_{303}) and among the seasons from 1.14 gms (pre-monsoon) to 1.20 gms (monsoon). The interaction between race and season revealed that MU_{303} in monsoon was found to record maximum cocoon weight (1.24 g) compared to others.

Table 1.7: Mean Performance of Cocoon Weight (Grams) in Multivoltine Races

Race (R)	Season (s)			Mean
	Pre-monsoon	Monsoon	Post-monsoon	
MU_1	1.20	1.23	1.22	1.22
MU_{11}	1.20	1.23	1.22	1.22
MU_{303}	1.19	1.24	1.23	1.22
PM	0.97	1.11	1.06	1.05
Mean	1.14	1.20	1.18	–

ANOVA

Source of variation	df	MSS	F ratio	CD at 5%
Replication	2	0.0002	0.60^{NS}	–
Season (S)	2	0.0111	28.29*	0.01
Race (R)	3	0.0649	164.84*	0.01
Interaction (S × R)	6	0.0023	5.97*	0.03
Error	22	0.0004		

* Significant.

NS: Non-significant.

The analysis of variance revealed that the cocoon weight was found to differ significantly ($P<0.05$) among races, seasons and also for interaction between season and race.

Shell Weight

Analysis of the data revealed that all the three new multivoltine races were observed to register higher shell weight compared to the control, PM (0.14 g) (Table 1.8). The mean values for this trait was found to vary, among the races from 0.18 g (MU_{11}) to 0.19 g (MU_{303}) and among the seasons from 0.16 g (pre-monsoon) to 0.18 g (monsoon). The interaction between the seasons and races revealed that MU_{303} in monsoon was found to register maximum shell weight (0.20 g) compared to others.

Table 1.8: Mean Performance of Shell Weight (Grams) in Multivoltine Races

Race (R)	Season (s)			Mean
	Pre-monsoon	Monsoon	Post-monsoon	
MU_1	0.17	0.19	0.18	0.18
MU_{11}	0.17	0.19	0.18	0.18
MU_{303}	0.17	0.20	0.19	0.19
PM	0.14	0.15	0.15	0.14
Mean	0.16	0.18	0.18	–

ANOVA

Source of variation	df	MSS	F ratio	CD at 5%
Replication	2	0.0000	0.19^{NS}	–
Season (S)	2	0.0011	40.19*	0.004
Race (R)	3	0.0030	109.61*	0.005
Interaction (S × R)	6	0.0001	5.22*	0.008
Error	22	0.0000		

* Significant.

NS: Non-significant.

The analysis of variance revealed that the trait was noticed to differ significantly ($P < 0.05$) among seasons, races and for interaction between season and race.

Shell Ratio

The observations recorded for shell ratio revealed that all the three new multivoltine races were found to be superior compared to the control, PM (14.23 %) (Table 1.9). The mean shell ratio was observed to vary, among the races from 15.04% (MU_1) to 15.52% (MU_{303}) and among the seasons from 14.49% (pre-monsoon) to 15.22% (monsoon). The interaction between race and season revealed that the race, MU_{303} was found to register maximum shell ratio (16.30%) in monsoon compared to others.

Table 1.9: Mean Performance of Shell Ratio (Percentage) in Multivoltine Races

Race (R)	Season (s)			Mean
	Pre-monsoon	Monsoon	Post-monsoon	
MU_1	14.56 (3.81)	15.31 (3.91)	15.26 (3.90)	15.04 (3.87)
MU_{11}	14.12 (3.75)	15.74 (3.96)	15.40 (3.92)	15.08 (3.88)
MU_{303}	14.18 (3.76)	16.30 (4.03)	16.09 (4.01)	15.52 (3.93)
PM	15.11 (3.88)	13.56 (3.68)	14.04 (3.74)	14.23 (3.77)
Mean	14.49 (3.80)	15.22 (3.90)	15.20 (3.89)	–

Note: Values in parentheses are angular transformed values.

ANOVA

Source of variation	df	MSS	F ratio	CD at 5%
Replication	2	0.0009	0.21^{NS}	–
Season (S)	2	0.0340	7.80*	0.05
Race (R)	3	0.0432	9.93*	0.06
Interaction (S × R)	6	0.0372	8.54*	0.11
Error	22	0.0044		–

* Significant.

NS: Non-significant.

The analysis of variance revealed that the trait was found to differ significantly (P <0.05) among races, seasons and also for interaction between season and race.

Silk Filament Length

Perusal of the data revealed that all the three new multivoltine races were found to be superior than the control, PM (416.44 m) (Table 1.10). The mean silk filament length was observed to vary among the races from 592.55m (MU_1) to 618.55 m (MU_{303}) and among the seasons from 530.83 mts (pre-monsoon) to 577.16mts (post-monsoon). The interaction between race and season revealed that MU_{303} was found to record maximum filament length (648.33 m) in post-monsoon compared to others.

Table 1.10: Mean Performance of Silk Filament Length (Meters) in Multivoltine Races

Race (R)	Season (s)			Mean
	Pre-monsoon	Monsoon	Post-monsoon	
MU_1	581.33	607.66	588.66	592.55
MU_{11}	579.00	620.00	636.33	611.77
MU_{303}	568.66	638.66	648.33	618.55
PM	394.33	419.66	435.33	416.44
Mean	530.83	571.49	577.15	–

ANOVA

Source of variation	df	MSS	F ratio	CD at 5%
Replication	2	59.5000	1.41^{NS}	–
Season (S)	2	7665.5000	181.92*	5.46
Race (R)	3	83333.0000	1977.69*	6.31
Interaction (S × R)	6	820.0000	19.46*	10.93
Error	22	42.1364		

* Significant.

NS: Non-significant

The analysis of variance revealed that the trait was found to differ significantly ($P < 0.05$) among races, seasons and also for interaction between season and race.

Pupation Rate

The results recorded for pupation rate revealed that all the three new multivoltine races were found to exhibit higher pupation rate compared to the control, PM (86.51%) (Table 1.11) . The mean pupation rate was observed to vary among the new races from 89.99% (MU_{303}) to 91.03% (MU_1) and among the seasons from 85.35% (pre-monsoon) to 94.00% (monsoon).

Table 1.11: Mean Performance of Pupation Rate (Percentage in Multivoltine Races

Race (R)	Season (s)			Mean
	Pre-monsoon	Monsoon	Post-monsoon	
MU_1	87.92 (9.37)	95.11 (9.75)	90.08 (9.49)	91.03 (9.54)
MU_{11}	85.88 (9.26)	96.03 (9.79)	89.88 (9.48)	90.59 (9.51)
MU_{303}	85.00 (9.21)	94.83 (9.73)	90.16 (9.49)	89.99 (9.48)
PM	82.63 (9.09)	90.05 (9.48)	86.86 (9.31)	86.51 (9.30)
Mean	85.35 (9.23)	94.00 (9.69)	89.24 (9.44)	–

Note: Values in parentheses are angular transformed values.

ANOVA

Source of variation	df	MSS	F ratio	CD at 5%
Replication	2	0.0005	0.04^{NS}	–
Season (S)	2	0.6576	61.87*	0.08
Race (R)	3	0.1074	10.59*	0.09
Interaction (S × R)	6	0.0073	0.71^{NS}	0.16
Error	22	0.0101		

* Significant.

NS: Non-significant.

The analysis of variance revealed that the trait was observed to differ significantly (P <0.05) among races and seasons. The interaction between the season and race was found to be non-significant (P >0.05).

The analysis of the data presented above reveal that all the three new multivoltine races were found to be superior than the control, PM with respect to all the eleven metric traits studied. However, significant differences (P< 0.05) were observed only for four traits namely: fecundity, hatching percentage, larval duration and filament length while the difference for other traits such as larval weight, cocoon yield by number, cocoon yield by weight, cocoon weight, shell weight, shell ratio and pupation rate was found to be non-significant (P>0.05). The interaction between season and race was found to be significant (P<0.05) only for the traits like cocoon weight, shell weight, shell ratio, filament length, larval weight and larval duration. MU_{303} was found to exhibit higher values for cocoon weight, shell weight and shell ratio during monsoon seasons; longer filament length during post-monsoon and higher larval weight in pre-monsoon season. While MU_{11} was found to record shorter larval duration during the monsoon season than the others.

BIVOLTINE RACES

Fecundity

Perusal of the data given in Table 1.12 revealed that the fecundity was found to be higher in MU_{852} (544.00) followed by MG_{414} (537.33). MG_{408} was found to register lower fecundity (523.77) compared to the control, NB_4D_2 (532.11). The mean fecundity among the seasons was found to vary from 531.66 (post-monsoon) to 538.16 (pre-monsoon).

The analysis of variance revealed that the trait was observed torecord non-significant (P>0.05) difference among races, seasons and for interaction between season and race.

Table 1.12: Mean Performance of Fecundity (Number) in Bivoltine Races

Race (R)	Season (s)			Mean
	Pre-monsoon	Monsoon	Post-monsoon	
MU_{852}	533.33 (23.09)	554.33 (23.54)	544.33 (23.33)	544.00 (23.22)
MG_{414}	537.66 (23.18)	540.00 (23.23)	534.33 (23.11)	537.33 (23.18)
MG_{408}	526.66 (22.94)	525.00 (22.91)	519.66 (22.79)	523.77 (22.88)
$NB_4 D_2$	555.00 (23.55)	513.00 (22.64)	528.33 (22.98)	532.11 (23.06)
Mean	538.16 (23.19)	533.08 (23.08)	531.66 (23.05)	–

Note: Values in parentheses are angular transformed values.

ANOVA

Source of variation	df	MSS	F ratio	CD at 5%
Replication	2	0.5586	4 47 NS	–
Season (S)	2	0.0645	0.51 NS	0.29
Race (R)	3	0.3079	2.46 NS	0.34
Interaction (S × R)	6	0.2507	2.00 NS	0.59
Error	22	0.1248		

NS: Non-significant.

Hatching Percentage

The analysis of the data given in Table 1.13 revealed that the hatching percentage was observed to be higher in all the three new bivoltine races compared to the control, NB_4D_2 (94.41%). The mean values for this traits was found to vary among the new races from 94.79% (MG_{408}) to 95.43% (MG_{414}) and among the seasons from 93.70% (pre-monsoon) to 95.95% (monsoon).

Table 1.13: Mean Performance of Hatching Percentage in Bivoltine Races

Race (R)	Season (s)			Mean
	Pre-monsoon	Monsoon	Post-monsoon	
MU_{852}	94.60 (9.72)	95.93 (9.79)	94.95 (9.74)	95.16 (9.75)
MG_{414}	94.37 (9.71)	96.95 (9.84)	94.98 (9.74)	95.43 (9.76)
MG_{408}	93.40 (9.66)	95.11 (9.75)	95.86 (9.79)	94.79 (9.73)
NB_4D_2	92.42 (9.61)	95.80 (9.78)	95.00 (9.74)	94.41 (9.71)
Mean	93.70 (9.67)	95.95 (9.79)	95.19 (9.75)	–

Note: Values in parentheses are angular transformed values.

ANOVA

Source of variation	df	MSS	F ratio	CD at 5%
Replication	2	0.0009	0.28 ^{NS}	0.04
Season (S)	2	0.0417	14.03 ^{NS}	0.04
Race (R)	3	0.0047	1.58 ^{NS}	0.05
Interaction (S × R)	6	0.0045	1.51 ^{NS}	0.09
Error	22	0.0030		

NS: Non-significant.

The analysis of variance revealed that the hatching percentage was observed to differ and non-significantly (P>0.05) among races and seasons and for interaction between season and race.

Larval Duration

The observations recorded revealed that all the three new bivoltine races were found to record higher larvel duration (Table 1.14) compared to the control, NB_4D_2 (575.00 h). The mean values were observed to vary, among the new races from 572.88 hrs (MG_{408}) to 573.88 hrs (MG_{414}) and among the seasons from 556.91 h (pre-monsoon) to 585.66 h (post-monsoon).

Table 1.14: Mean Performance of Larval Duration (Hours) in Bivoltine Races

Race (R)	Season (s)			Mean
	Pre-monsoon	Monsoon	Post-monsoon	
MU_{852}	555.33 (23.56)	576.00 (24.00)	585.66 (24.20)	572.33 (23.92)
MG_{414}	553.66 (23.53)	576.00 (24.00)	592.00 (24.33)	573.88 (23.951)
MG_{408} (23.93)	557.00 (23.60)	577.66 (24.03)	584.00 (24.16)	572.88 (24.16)
NB_4 D_2	561.66 (23.69)	582.33 (24.13)	581.00 (24.10)	575.00 (23.97)
Mean	556.91 (23.59)	578.00 (24.04)	585.66 (24.20)	–

Note: Values in parentheses are angular transformed values.

ANOVA

Source of variation	df	MSS	F ratio	CD at 5%
Replication	2	0.0352	1.17^{NS}	–
Season (S)	2	1.1621	38.72 *	0.14
Race (R)	3	0.0046	0.15^{NS}	0.16
Interaction (S × R)	6	0.0254	0.84^{NS}	0.29
Error	22	0.0300		

* Significant.

NS: Non-significant

The analysis of variance revealed that the larval duration was found to vary significantly (P< 0.05) among seasons and non-significantly (P>0.05) among races and for interaction between season and race.

Larval Weight

Perusal of the data given in Table 1.15 revealed that the larval weight was found to be higher for MU_{852} (44.97 gms), NB_4D_2 (44.38 g) and MG_{414} (44.32 g) compared to MG_{408} (43.85 g). It was observed to register higher larval weight in post-monsoon (46.93 g) followed by monsoon (44.28 g) and pre-monsoon (41.92 g).

The analysis of variance revealed that the trait was noticed to differ significantly ($P<0.05$) among seasons and races, non-significantly for interaction between season and race.

Table 1.15: Mean Performance of Larval Weight (Grams) in Bivoltine Races

Race (R)	Season (s)			Mean
	Pre-monsoon	Monsoon	Post-monsoon	
MU_{852}	42.53	45.40	47.00	44.97
MG_{414}	41.89	43.83	47.25	44.32
MG_{408}	41.04	44.10	46.43	43.85
$NB_4 D_2$	42.25	43.82	47.07	44.38
Mean	41.92	44.28	46.93	–

Note: Values in parentheses are angular transformed values.

ANOVA

Source of variation	df	MSS	F ratio	CD at 5%
Replication	2	0.6445	1.25^{NS}	–
Season (S)	2	75.4180	146.66 *	0.60
Race (R)	3	1.9063	3.70*	0.69
Interaction (S × R)	6	0.7083	1.37^{NS}	1.20
Error	22	0.5142		

* Significant.

NS: Non-significant

Cocoon Yield by Number

The results obtained for cocoon yield by number (Table 1.16) revealed that all the three new bivoltine races were observed to record higher cocoon yield by number than the control, NB_4D_2 (8659.10). The mean values were found to vary, among the new races from 8790.00 (MU_{852}) to 8956.66 (MG_{414}) and among the seasons from 8398.16 (pre-monsoon) to 9023.49 (post-monsoon).

Table 1.16: Mean Performance of Cocoon Yield by Number in Bivoltine Races

Race (R)	Season (s)			Mean
	Pre-monsoon	Monsoon	Post-monsoon	
MU_{852}	8245.00 (90.80)	9000.00 (90.80)	9125.00 (95.52)	8790.00 (93.75)
MG_{414}	8556.66 (92.50)	9030.00 (95.02)	9283.33 (96.35)	8956.66 (94.63)
MG_{408}	8459.33 (91.97)	9007.33 (94.90)	9013.33 (94.93)	8826.66 (93.95)
$NB_4 D_2$	8331.66 (91.27)	8973.33 (94.72)	8672.33 (93.12)	8659.10 (93.05)
Mean	8398.16 (91.64)	9002.66 (94.88)	9023.49 (91.64)	–

Note: Values in parentheses are angular transformed values.

ANOVA

Source of variation	df	MSS	F ratio	CD at 5%
Replication	2	0.3594	0.42 NS	–
Season (S)	2	43.3750	50.97*	0.77
Race (R)	3	3.8542	4.52*	0.89
Interaction (S × R)	6	1.7969	2.11 NS	1.55
Error	22	0.8509		

* Significant.

NS: Non-significant.

The analysis of variance revealed that the cocoon yield by number was found to differ significantly (P<0.05) among races, seasons and the interaction between season and race was found to be non-significant (P>0.05).

Cocoon Yield by Weight

The analysis of data given in Table 1.17 revealed that MG_{408} was found to record higher cocoon yield by weight (15.01 kg) followed by MG_{414} (14.94 kg) and NB_4D_2 (14.65 kg). MU_{852} was found to record lesser cocoon yield by weight (14.50 kg) compared to the control NB_4D_2 (14.65 kg). It was observed to register higher values (15.40 kg) in post-monsoon followed by monsoon (15.24 kg) and pre-monsoon seasons (13.69 kg). The interaction between the race and season revealed that MG_{414} was found to record maximum cocoon yield by weight (15.93 kg) in post-monsoon season compared to others.

Table 1.17: Mean Performance of Cocoon Yield by Weight (Kilograms) in Bivoltine Races

Race (R)	Season (s)			Mean
	Pre monsoon	Monsoon	Post-monsoon	
MU_{852}	13.38	14.81	15.32	14.50
MG_{414}	14.00	14.90	15.93	14.94
MG_{408}	13.73	15.76	15.56	15.01
NB_4D_2	13.66	15.49	14.82	14.65
Mean	13.69	15.24	15.40	–

ANOVA

Source of variation	df	MSS	F ratio	CD at 5%
Replication	2	0.1321	0.91 NS	–
Season (S)	2	10.7239	74.61*	0.31
Race (R)	3	0.5197	3.61*	0.36
Interaction (S × R)	6	0.4773	3.32 *	0.63
Error	22	0.1437		

* Significant.

NS: Non-significant.

The analysis of variance revealed that the cocoon yield by weight was found to differ significantly ($P<0.05$) among races, seasons and for interaction between season and race.

Cocoon Weight

Perusal of the data given in Table 1.18 revealed that MG_{408} was found to register higher cocoon weight (1.70 g) followed by NB_4D_2 (1.67 g). It was observed to be marginally lower in the races, MU_{852} (1.65 g) and MG_{414} (1.67 or 1.668) compared to the control, NB_4D_2 (1.67 g). Monsoon season was found to register higher mean cocoon weight (1.69 g) followed by post-monsoon (1.69 g) and pre-monsoon (1.63 g). The interaction between race and season revealed that MG_{408} was observed to register maximum cocoon weight (1.75 g) in monsoon season.

Table 1.18: Mean Performance of Cocoon Weight (Grams) in Bivoltine Races

Race (R)	Season (s)			Mean
	Pre-monsoon	Monsoon	Post-monsoon	
MU_{852}	1.623	1.647	1.680	1 .650
MG_{414}	1.637	1.650	1.717	1.668
MG_{408}	1.623	1.750	1.727	1.700
NB_4D_2	1.643	1.727	1.647	1.672
Mean	1.631	1.693	1.692	–

ANOVA

Source of variation	df	MSS	F ratio	CD at 5%
Replication	2	0.0020	1.47^{NS}	–
Season (S)	2	0.0150	11.15*	0.03
Race (R)	3	0.0039	2.86 ^{NS}	0.03
Interaction (S × R)	6	0.0044	3.28*	0.06
Error	22	0.0013		

* Significant.

NS: Non-significant.

The analysis of variance revealed that the cocoon weight was observed to vary non-significantly (P>0.05) among races and significantly (P<0.05) for seasons and for interaction between season and race.

Shell Weight

The results recorded for shell weight revealed that all the three new bivoltine races were found to register higher shell weight than the control, NB_4D_2 (0.306g) (Table 1.19). MG_{408} was found to register higher mean shell weight (0.314 g) followed by MG_{414} (0.311 g) and MU_{852} (0.307 g). In pre-monsoon season shell weight was observed to be higher (0.322 g) followed by monsoon (0.308 g) and post-monsoon (0.299 g). The interaction between the race and season revealed that the race, MU_{852} in pre-monsoon was observed to register maximum shell weight (0.328 g or 0.33 g).

Table 1.19: Mean Performance of Shell Weight (Grams) in Bivoltine Races

Race (R)	Season (s)			Mean
	Pre-monsoon	Monsoon	Post-monsoon	
MU_{852}	0.328	0.295	0.299	0.307
MG_{414}	0.321	0.304	0.308	0.311
MG_{408}	0.319	0.320	0.305	0.314
NB_4D_2	0.322	0.313	0.285	0.306
Mean	0.322	0.308	0.299	–

ANOVA

Source of variation	df	MSS	F ratio	CD at 5%
Replication	2	0.0000	1.17 NS	–
Season (S)	2	0.0017	40.45*	0.005
Race (R)	3	0.0001	3.35*	0.006
Interaction (S × R)	6	0.0003	7.24*	0.01
Error	22	0.0000		

* Significant.

NS: Non-significant.

The analysis of variance revealed that the shell weight was found to vary non-significantly (P>0.05) among races and significantly (P<0.05) among seasons and for interaction between season and race.

Shell Ratio

Perusal of the data given in Table 1.20 revealed that the shell ratio was observed to be higher for the three new biovoltine races compared to the control, NB_4D_2 (18.32 %). The mean values for this trait was found to vary among the new races from 18.55% (MG_{408}) to 18.66% (MG_{414}) and among the seasons from 17.67% post-monsoon to 19.77% (pre-monsoon).

Table 1.20: Mean Performance of Shell Ratio (Percentage) in Bivoltine Races

Race (R)	Season (s)			Mean
	Pre-monsoon	Monsoon	Post-monsoon	
MU_{852}	20.22 (4.49)	17.91 (4.49)	17.81 (4.22)	18.64 (4.31)
MG_{414}	19.61 (4.42)	18.45 (4.29)	17.94 (4.23)	18.66 (4.32)
MG_{408}	19.67 (4.43)	18.30 (4.27)	17.68 (4.20)	18.55 (4.30)
NB_4D_2	19.58 (4.42)	18.10 (4.25)	17.28 (4.15)	18.32 (4.28)
Mean	19.77 (4.44)	18.19 (4.26)	17.67 (4.20)	–

Note: Values in parentheses are angular transformed values.

ANOVA

Source of variation	df	MSS	F ratio	CD at 5%
Replication	2	0.0001	0.0552 NS	–
Season (S)	2	0.1903	114.69*	0.03
Race (R)	3	0.0031	1.86NS	0.03
Interaction (S × R)	6	0.0030	1.82 Ns	0.06
Error	22	0.0017		

* Significant.

NS: Non-significant.

The analysis of variance revealed that the shell weight was found to vary significantly ($p < 0.05$) among seasons and non-significantly ($P > 0.05$) among races and for interaction between seasons and race.

Silk Filament Length

The results obtained for silk filament length revealed that MG_{414} was found to register longer silk filament length (982.55 m) followed by the control, NB_4D_2 (979.66 m) (Table 1.21). The mean for this trait was observed to be shorter in the races MU_{852} (972.77 m) and MG_{408} (977.10 m) compared to the control, NB_4D_2 (979.66 m). The mean silk filament length was found to be longer in monsoon (993.32 mts) followed by pre-monsoon (982.08 m) and post-monsoon season (958.66 m).

Table 1.21: Mean Performance of Silk Filament Length (Metres) in Bivoltine Races

Race (R)	Season (s)			Mean
	Pre-monsoon	Monsoon	Post-monsoon	
MU_{852}	989.00	976.66	952.66	972.77
MG_{414}	987.33	993.33	967.00	982.55
MG_{408}	971.33	1006.66	953.33	977.10
NB_4D_2	980.66	996.66	961.66	979.66
Mean	982.08	933.32	958.66	–

ANOVA

Source of variation	df	MSS	F ratio	CD at 5%
Replication	2	362.00	1.92 Ns	–
Season (S)	2	3892.00	20.74*	11.54
Race (R)	3	166.66	0.88 NS	11.32
Interaction (S × R)	6	331.33	1.76 Ns	23.08
Error	22	187.63		

* Significant.

NS: Non-significant.

The analysis of variance revealed that the filament length was observed to vary significantly ($P<0.05$) among seasons and non-significantly ($p>0.05$) among races and for interaction between season and race.

Pupation Rate

The observations recorded for this trait revealed that all the three new biovoltine races were found to express higher pupation rate compared to the control, NB_4D_2 (88.34%) (Table 1.22) . The mean values for the trait was observed to vary among the new races from 88.39% (MU_{852}) to 89.51% (MG_{414}) and among the seasons from 87.57% (pre-monsoon) to 89.78% (post-monsoon).

Table 1.22: Mean Performance of Pupation Rate (Percentage) in Bivoltine Races

Race (R)	Season (s)			Mean
	Pre-monsoon	Monsoon	Post-monsoon	
MUH_{852}	86.22 (9.28)	89.30 (9.44)	89.67 (9.46)	88.39 (9.40)
MG_{414}	87.49 (9.35)	89.16 (9.44)	91.88 (9.58)	89.51 (9.46)
MG_{408}	88.87 (9.42)	88.83 (9.42)	88.93 (9.43)	88.87 (9.42)
NB_4D_2	87.72 (9.36)	88.66 (9.41)	88.66 (9.41)	88.34 (9.39)
Mean	87.57 (9.35)	88.98 (9.43)	89.78 (9.47)	–

Note: Values in parentheses are angular transformed values.

ANOVA

Source of variation	df	MSS	F ratio	CD at 5%
Replication	2	0.0159	3.46 NS	–
Season (S)	2	0.0428	9.34*	0.05
Race (R)	3	0.0074	1.61 NS	0.06
Interaction (S x R)	6	0.0106	2.30 NS	0.11
Error	22	0.0046		

* Significant.

NS: Non-significant.

The analysis of variance revealed that the pupation rate was found to vary significantly ($P<0.05$) among seasons and non-significantly ($P>0.05$) among races and for interaction between season and race.

The analysis of the data on the performance of the three new bivoltine races and control NB_4D_2 was observed that they were found to exhibit marginal differences over the control NB_4D_2 for the characters viz. fecundity, hatching percentage, larval duration, cocoon weight, shell weight, shell ratio, filament length and pupation rate. While all the three new races were found to exhibit significant variation for the characters like larval weight, cocoon yield by number, cocoon yield by weight. The cocoon yield by number was found to be observed significantly higher in new races compared to the control, NB_4D_2. Cocoon yield by weight was found to be higher in MG_{414}, MG_{408} compared to other two races. Characters like cocoon yield by number, cocoon yield by weight, cocoon weight, pupation rate were found to be expressed favourably during monsoon and post-monsoon seasons. While shell weight and shell ratio were observed to be manifested favourably during pre-monsoon. The character, filament length was observed to record longer length during monsoon and pre-monsoon season compared to post-monsoon. The interaction between seasons and race revealed that only three characters such as cocoon yield by weight, single cocoon weight and single shell weight were found to exhibit the seasonal interaction. Cocoon yield by weight was found to be significantly higher in MG_{414} during post-monsoon. While cocoon weight was found to be significantly higher for MG_{408} during monsoon. Similarly single shell weight was found to be significantly more in MU_{852} during pre-monsoon. The other characters were found to express independent to season.

DISCUSSION

Evaluation of the data pertaining to eleven economic traits presented in Tables 1.1 to 1.11 for multivoltine races and Tables 1.12 to 1.22 for bivoltine races exhibit a typical picture of genotype and environmental interactions. The varied responses in the expression of eleven metric traits in different silkworm races to the prevailing environmental conditions during the period of rearing clearly demonstrates the genetic architecture of the races as well their interaction with different environmental conditions. The magnitude in the phenotypic variability is dependent on the responsiveness of the different genotypes to different environmental conditions. Such studies are well documented in both plants and animals (Griffing and Zsioros, 1971; Orozco, 1976 and Strickberger, 1976). In addition,, the variability observed for different traits in different silkworm races is in conformity with the studies made by Finlay and Wilkinson (1963), Eberhart and Russel (1966), Perkins and Jinks (1968), Samuel *et al.*, (1970), Freeman and Perkins (1971), Harada (1961) who demonstrated the phonomenon convincingly. It is well known that the dynamic environmental conditions prevailing in different seasons of the year bring about profound changes in the physical and biotic factors influencing the growth and development as well the phenotypic expression of many economic traits, (Kogura, 1932; Suzuki, 1954; Narayanan et al, 1967; Ueda et al., 1969; Krishnaswami et al., 1970a, 1970b; Kobayashi et al., 1986 and Muslim, 1986). It is understood that the performance of a race or a breed is mainly dependent on the combined action of hereditary potential of its population and the extent to which such potential is permitted to express in the environment to which it is exposed. The differential expression of different races in different seasons recorded in the present study is in conformity with the observations of Hassanein and Sharawwy, 1962; Kashiviswanathan *et al.*, 1970, Ananymous, 1971; Krishnaswamy and Narasimhanna, 1974; and Ueda et al., 1975. This is largely due to the variable gene frequencies at different loci in different silkworm races which make them to respond differently to changing environmental conditions and parallels the findings of Watanabe, 1918 and 1919; Fukuda 1960; Fukuda *et al.*, 1963; Morohoshi, 1969; Sengupta, 1969 and 1988;Ueda *et al.*,1969; Subramanya, 1985; Kalpana, 1992; Kalappa, 1996; Nanjundaswamy, 1997.

The highest values observed for majority of the traits viz. fecundity, hatching percentage, larval weight, cocoon yield by number, cocoon yield by weight, single cocoon weight, single shell weight, shell ratio, filament length and pupation rate for all the races under study in monsoon and post-monsoon seasons and lower values observed for the above traits in pre-monsoon season indicates the positive/ negative response of the respective genotypes to favourable/ unfavourable rearing environmental conditions prevailing during the different seasons is in conformity with the earlier findings of Jaroonchi, 1972; Narasimhanna, 1976; Subramanya, 1985; Rajanna, 1989; Raju, 1990; Maribashetty, 1991; Kalpana, 1992; Nanjundaswamy, 1997 and Veeraiah, 1999. The study clearly demonstrates the complexity of the polygenic inheritance of the economic traits in silkworm.

The higher fecundity recorded for all the races under study than the respective controls can be attributed to the genetic potential. Similarly higher fecundity observed in monsoon and post-monsoon seasons indicate their favourable response to the conditions prevailing in those two seasons (Tables 1.1 and 1.12). The reduced larval duration exhibited by both multivoltine and bivoltine races compared to respective control reflect their better genotypic response for faster growth and development (1.3 and 1.14). However, slightly longer larval duration observed during post-monsoon season can be attributed to the reduced rate of metabolism resulting in slow growth rate due to lower temperature and other associated environmental conditions (Yokoyama, 1962 and Morohoshi , 1969). The higher larval weight exhibited by both multivoitine and bivoltine races than the respective controls can be ascribed to their favourable genetic response. The superiority in effective rate of rearing as evidenced by the cocoon yield by number in both multivoitine and bivoltine races can be attributed to the favourable combination of genes exhibiting a positive response to the changing environmental conditions in the expression of the trait. Similarly the highest mean values for this trait observed in different seasons indicate higher viability compared to the respective controls.

In addition, higher values observed for the productivity traits such as cocoon yield by weight, cocoon weight, shell weight and shell ratio in both multivolitne and bivoitine races (Tables 1.6 to 1.19 and Tables 1.17 to 1.20) than the respective control confirm their superiority. Similarly the longer filament length exhibited by both new multivoltines and new bivoltine races clearly indicate the superiority of the gene combinations present in the races.

The overall superiority observed in the expression of the most of the economic traits analysed in new multivoitine and new bivoltine races over their respective controls in different seasons of the year confer their genetic advantages over the respective controls. All the three new multivoitine and bivoltine races selected for the study, thus prove their superiority under the tropical conditions prevailing in Rayalaseema region.

As pointed out by Barton (1986) nothing is known about the genetic basis of quantitative characters except for measuring phenotypic variance and environmental components. The complex interaction between the blocks of polygenes and the environmental conditions is a phenomenon, which has been studied in many plants and animals. However, still precise information on this aspect is wanting. Even the molecular biology has failed to throw light on this important phenomenon. Therefore, it can be concluded that the performance of the races in question and their superiority over their respective controls could be due to favorable gene complexes and their interaction during growth and development leading to the phenotypic improvement as evidenced by the data analyzed for eleven metric traits.

SUMMARY

1. The performance of the three new multivoltine races MU_1, MU_{11}, MU_{303} and three new bivoltine races MU_{852}, MG_{414}, MG_{408} procured from the germplasm bank maintained in the university of Mysore was evaluated by rearing them in different seasons of the year along with their respective controls, PM and NB_4D_2. They were evaluated on the basis of the expression of eleven metric traits such as fecundity, hatching percentage, larval duration, larval weight, cocoon yield by number, cocoon yield by weight, cocoon weight, shell weight, shell ratio, filament length and pupation rate, studied in three different seasons.

2. The data obtained were pooled separately for multivoltine and bivoltine races and was subjected to relevant statistical methods to understand the interaction between the races and the seasons.

3. Majority of the characters studied were found to record higher values during the favorable seasons, monsoon and post-monsoon than the unfavourable season, pre-monsoon. Further, interestingly all the three multivoltine and the three bivoltine races were observed to register superiority over their respective controls. The superiority with regard to their viability and productivity is a noteworthy feature. The interaction between the races and seasons was found to be prominently seen in the expression of the characters like, larval duration, larval weight, cocoon yield by weight, shell weight, shell ratio and filament length.

4. The results of the evaluation clearly indicate that the three new multivoltine and three bivoltine races were

found to excel their respective controls exhibiting their superiority, which could be attributed to their genetic advantage. Further, they confer their superiority by their positive response to the environmental conditions prevailing in Rayalaseema region. The marginal differences observed in the expression the eleven economic traits studied among the new races could be attributed to their genetic differences. However, the over all superiority of the new races under study has enabled to select them as parental races to be used in the hybridization programme in order to develop promising hybrids for commercial exploitation.

Chapter 2

EVALUATION OF THE GENETIC POTENTIAL OF MULTI-BIHYBRIDS AND THE IDENTIFICATION OF PROMISING HYBRIDS

INTRODUCTION

The aim of silkworm breeding is not only to synthesize new genotypes but also to identify suitable hybrid combinations for commercial exploitation. Even though, the inbred lines are superior, they do not have much value, if they do not exhibit superiority when they are crossed. Therefore, ultimate results in silkworm breeding are judged by the excellency of the commercial traits of the parental races that appear in F_1 hybrids. Cross-breeding of different strains usually produce more vigorous hybrid offsprings than either of the parental strains considered separately (or) their off-springs. This superiority is termed as "Heterosis" or "Hybrid vigour" may exhibit in itself the improved general fitness characters such as viability, productivity, disease resistance, uniformity in morphological characters, etc. The phenomenon of hybrid vigour has received considerable attention among biologists due to the marked improvement in productivity.

Many silkworm breeders in Japan practised crossing of different silkworm varieties without the knowledge of heterosis to improve the productivity. The first cross was made between Japanese multivoltive spring variety and a bivoltine summer variety and succeeded in breeding improved races for commercial exploitation. Later on Japanese silkworm varieties were crossed to Chinese and European varieties to breed superior silkworm races. About 50 different hybrids were produced for a period of 120 years from 1790 to 1910 without the knowledge of heterosis or hybrid vigour (Osawa, 1936 and Hiratsuka, 1969). The hybrids derived from crossing silkworm varieties of Chinese and Japanese origin became very popular with the farmers. By 1919 over 90 per cent of the eggs produced were of hybrid origin and by 1928 the utilization of hybrids for commercial exploitation reached 100 per cent (Yokoyama, 1973). The average weight of cocoon shell which was about 20 cg in 1904 was gradually increased and reached over 40 cg in 1932 and to 60 cg in 1960 (Hirobe, 1985). Similarly, other characters such as fecundity, hatching percentage, viability, filament length and fibre qualities were improved as a result of continuous efforts made by silkworm breeders in adjudicating the highly promising F_1 hybrids for commercial exploitation. In fact the exploitation of hybrid vigour heralded a new era in sericulture which contributed substantially to the increased silk production in Japan (Toyama, 1905, 1906a, 1906b; Osawa and Harada, 1944; Katsumata, 1948; Yokoyama, 1957, 1974; Petkov, 1975; Petkov *et al.*, 1979, 1982; Petkov and Yolov, 1980). Similarly several productive hybrids were developed in other sericultural countries such as China, then USSR and South Korea to improve the silk production (Strunnikov, 1971 and Abadjieva and Radka, 1980).

However, in India utilization of hybrid vigour came rather late during 1920s. Since the parental strains involved in the hybrids were multivoltine races with poor qualitative and quantitative characters, the hybrids produced could not contribute to the rapid progress in productivity. Inspite of this, the hybrids of multivoltine Pure Mysore and bivoltine race, *C. nichi* became popular with the farmers because of the consistency in crop stability (Nanavathy, 1965). The cross breeding of silkworm races was initiated systematically during 1960s by utilizing multivoltine Pure Mysore with exotic bivoltine races such as J_{112}, C_{108} and NN_6D (Jolly, 1983). Even though these hybrids were found to be superior over the multivoltine parent Pure Mysore, expected goals of achieving the desired objective of increasing the productivity could not be fully realized as a result of inherent defects of multivoltine Pure Mysore that are passed on to the hybrids (Tazima, 1958). Mean while some of the exotic bivoltine races turned into multivoltines due to improper maintenance and deteriorated considerably resulting in poor hybrid vigour in F_1 hybrids. Inspite of this the use of these exotic races as male parents in the cross breeding programme with Pure Mysore race was continued in the preparation of hybrids without much progress. Later on cross breeding programme was initiated by utilizing the new bivoltine breeds such as KA, NB_7, NB_{18} and NB_4D_2 developed in India as a male component to cross with Pure Mysore race (Narasimhanna *et al.*, 1976 and Krishnaswami, 1978). The above hybrids were found to be superior and contributed a great deal in increasing the cocoon production (Singh and Hirobe, 1964; Krishnaswami and Narashimhanna, 1974 and Benchamin *et al.*, 1988). However the quality of the silk produced from these hybrids remains to be poor since the inherent defects of multivioltine races are passed on to their hybrids. Since then several attempts were made to identify different combinations of multi □ bi F_1, hybrids under Karnataka conditions, without much success (Tikoo *et al.*, 1971; Benchamin *et al.*, 1988; Datta and Pershad, 1988; Raje Urs; 1988, Subba Rao and Sahai, 1989; Raju, 1990; Chandrashekaraiah, 1992; Kalpana, 1992; Kalappa, 1996 and Veeraiah 1999).

The sericulture practices in Rayalaseema region of Andhra Pradesh is largely dependent on the technologies developed and practised in Karnataka. Therefore, the multi bi hybrids which are popular in Karnataka are being commercially exploited in Rayalaseema region. Over a period of time out of four promising multi × bi hybrids namely, PM × KA, PM × NB_7, PM × NB_{18} and PM × NB_4D_2 only PM × NB_4D_2 is being exploited at present. While the other three no longer remain in the field due to their deterioration. As a result of this the growth and development of sericulture in that region is not in commensurate with time. Further, sincere efforts to develop promising commercial hybrids for that region is wanting. In order to strengthen the processing sericulture development in Andhra Pradesh it is necessary to develop silkworm breeds suitable to different climatic complexes and seasons of Rayalaseema region, where, sericultural activity is concentrated. Therefore, it is imperative to satisfy the requirement of highly promising F_1 hybrids. Due to the continuos effort of silkworm breeders in the country a large number of silkworm races have been made available. However, these races have not been exploited commercially as there is no systematic approach to identify promising hybrid combinations. In view of this and the multitude of choices, decisions, procedures and techniques kept at the disposal of silkworm breeders an attempt is made by utilizing three new multi voltine races MU_1, MU_{11} and MU_{303} and three new bivoltine races MU_{852}, MG_{414} and MG_{408} to synthesize new promising multi X bi hybrid combinations.

A reliable Line × Tester analysis developed by Kempthorne (1957) in which crossing of a set of females of several inbred lines to a common male parent is involved was employed to study the combining ability. This method enables to analyse the relative capacity of the female and male parents to produce hybrids. This is a very common method and utilized extensively in both plants and animals by several workers such as Setty and Singh, 1977; Kadkol *et al.*, 1984 in Sunflower, White and Richmond 1963; Singh *et al.*, 1971; Kaushik *et al*, 1984 in cotton; Rao *et al.*, 1968; Rana and Murthy, 1971 in Sorghum; Narasimhanna, 1976; Petkov *et al.*, 1982; Subba Rao, 1983; Raje Urs, 1988; Raju, 1990; Chandrashekaraiah, 1992; Kalpana, 1992; Malik, 1992; Nirmal Kumar, 1995; Kalappa, 1996; Veeraiah, 1999 in Silkworm.

The Line × Tester analysis enable to understand the genetic worth of the strains by evaluating the general combining ability (gca) of the parents and specific combining ability (sca) of the hybrids (Sprague and Tatum, 1942). Besides, it is important to understand the heterosis and over-dominance expressed in the hybrids to substantiate the genetic advantage of the hybrids in question. The degree of expression of heterosis and over-dominance in silkworm was also evaluated in the derived hybrid combinations in order to identify superior hybrid combinations.

It is well-known that identification of superior F_1 hybrids coupled with improved rearing practices have made possible to achieve the maximum biological efficiency such as reproductive rate, morphological uniformity, high tolerance to environmental disturbances, high viability and increased cocoon shell and shell percentage contributing to productivity. Keeping in view of the advantages of the heterotic effect, efforts have been made to maximize this phenomenon in the hybrids. Important commercial characteristics such as fecundity, hatching percentage, larval duration, larval weight, cocoon yield by number, cocoon yield by weight, cocoon weight, shell weight, shell percentage, silk filament length and pupation rate of the pure races and the hybrids were analysed by subjecting the data for appropriate statistical analysis. Further, the general combining ability of the pure races, the specific combining ability as well degree of heterosis and over dominance of hybrids were evaluated for each one of the eleven economic characters. On the basis of the results, superior hybrid combinations were identified for commercial exploitation.

MATERIAL AND METHODS

Three new mutivoltine races viz., MU_1, MU_{11}, MU_{303} and three new bivoltine races viz., MU_{852}, MG_{414}, MG_{408}, along with their respective control Pure Mysore and NB_4D_2 were utilized in the study to understand the degree of hetorisis, overdominance, general combining ability and specific combining ability by employing Line ⊠ Tester analysis. A total of sixteen hybrids were derived from four lines and four testers. All the hybrids and their parents were reared in replication of three by following the standard rearing techniques as described in Chapter 1. The data on the rearing performance of the hybrids as well the parental races with respect to eleven economic character such as fecundity, hatching percentage, larval duration, larval weight, cocoon yield by number, cocoon yield by weight, cocoon weight, shell weight, shell percentage, silk filament length and pupation rate were evaluated. The data generated was pooled separately for parental races and the hybrids and subjected to relevant statistical analysis in order to evaluate the performance of the parents as well the degree of manifestation of heterosis and over dominance in the hybrids with respect to each one of the traits. In addition, general combining ability of lines and testers as well as specific combining ability of the hybrids were evaluated to understand the ability of the new lines to cross with the new testers to yield profitable amounts of hybrid vigour. Simultaneously, the performance of the new multi ⊠ bi hybrids was compared with the control hybrid in the expression of eleven economic characters.

Statistical Procedures

The general combining ability of the lines and testers was estimated by employing the statistical method suggested by Kempthorne, (1957) as detailed below:

(a) Lines

$$g_1 = \frac{X_i}{tr} - \frac{X}{l_{tr}}$$

(b) Tester

$$g_t = \frac{X_j}{1_r} - \frac{X}{1_{tr}}$$

Where

1 = number of lines

t = number of testers and

r = number of replications

Similarly, specific combining ability of the hybrids involving lines and testers were estimated by applying the following statistical method of Kempthorne (1957).

$$S_{ij} = \frac{X_{ij}}{r} - \frac{X_i}{tr}, \frac{X_j}{tr} + \frac{X}{1_{tr}}$$

Standard errors for combining ability effects.

$$\text{S.E (gca for line)} = \left(\frac{me}{r} xt\right)^{\frac{1}{2}}$$

$$\text{S.E (gca for tester)} = \left(\frac{me}{r} x1\right)^{\frac{1}{2}}$$

$$\text{S.E (sca effects)} = \left(\frac{me}{r}\right)^{\frac{1}{2}}$$

$$\text{S.E } (g_i - g_j) \text{ line} = \left(\frac{2me}{r} x\right)^{\frac{1}{2}}$$

$$\text{S.E } (g_i - g_j) \text{ tester} = \left(\frac{2me}{r} xr\right)^{\frac{1}{2}}$$

$$\text{S.E } (S_{ij} - S_{kl}) = \left(\frac{2me}{r}\right)^{\frac{1}{2}}$$

The degree of heterosis and over dominance with respect to each one of the traits were calculated by the applications of the following formula:

$$\text{Heterosis} = \frac{F_1 - MPV}{MPV} \times 100$$

$$\text{Over dominance} = \frac{F_1 - BPV}{BPV} \times 100$$

Where,

F_1 = Mean of the hybrid

MPV = Mid parental value

BPV = Better parental value

RESULTS

The mean data pertaining to eleven economic traits of the parents and the hybrids are presented in Tables 2.1 and 2.2 respectively. The analysis of variance computed for the traits of the parents as well the hybrids is presented in Table 2.3. General combining ability estimate of the parents and the specific combining ability of the hybrids are presented in Tables 2.4 and 2.5 respectively. The sources of variation and the statistical values obtained for both general and specific combining abilities are presented in Table 2.6. The degree of manifestation of heterosis and over dominance is presented in Tables 2.7 and 2.8 respectively.

Table 2.1: Mean Performance of Parental Races for Eleven Economic Characters

Parental races	Fecundity (number)	Hatching percentage	Larval duration (hours)	Larval weight (grams)	Cocoon yield by number	Cocoon yield by weight (kg)	Cocoon weight (grams)	Shell weight (grams)	Shell ratio (%)	Filament Length (metres)	Pupation Rate (%)
1	2	3	4	5	6	7	8	9	10	11	12
Multivoltine											
MU_1	468.22	94.54	559.33	33.74	9214.32	11.26	1.222	0.184	15.04	592.55	91.03
MU_{11}	478.77	96.32	554.66	33.57	9155.21	11.17	1.220	0.184	15.08	611.77	90.60
MU_{303}	477.66	95.00	565.33	33.34	9125.66	11.18	1.225	0.190	15.52	618.55	90.00
PM	394.44	87.98	664.66	26 70	8739.11	9.17	1.053	0.150	14.24	416.44	86.51
Bivoltine											
MU_{852}	544.00	95.16	572.53	44 97	8790.00	14.66	1.680	0.307	18.64	982.77	88.39
MG_{414}	537.33	94.43	573.88	44.32	8956.66	14.94	1.668	0.311	18.66	982.55	89.51
MG_{408}	532.77	94.79	572.88	44.85	8826.66	15.01	1.700	0.314	18.55	987.11	88.83
NB_4D_2	532.11	94.41	575.00	43.38	8656.10	14.65	1.672	0.306	18.32	980.66	38.35

Table 2.2: Mean Performance of the Sixteen Hybrids for Eleven Economic Characters

Hybrids	Fecundity (number)	Hatching Percentage	Larval duration (hours)	Larval weight (grams)	Cocoon yield by number	Cocoon yield by weight (kg)	Cocoon weight (grams)	Shell weight (grams)	Shell ratio (%)	Filament length (metres)	Pupation rate (%)
1	2	3	4	5	6	7	8	9	10	11	12
$MU_1 \times MU_{852}$	476.00	93.74	539.33	39.81	8687.70	16.50	1.901	0.318	16.74	868.77	85.54
$MU_1 \times MG_{414}$	480.55	95.00	534.77	40.14	8723.66	15.82	1.818	0.299	16.44	856.55	86.08
$MU_1 \times MIG_{408}$	473.44	94.97	536.00	39.88	8533.22	15.67	1.834	0.293	15.97	828.11	84.14
$MU_1 \times NB_4D_2$	451.77	95.52	528.66	39.98	8829.44	16.07	1.820	0.290	15.97	834.00	87.37
$MU_{11} \times MU_{852}$	482.11	94.72	532.00	40.30	8778.00	15.80	1.789	0.304	17.01	860.44	86.32
$MU_{11} \times MG_{414}$	479.66	95.52	536.66	38.44	8651.66	15.99	1.847	0.297	16.09	819.88	85.26
$MU_{11} \times MG_{408}$	482.11	94.43	536.00	40.19	8714.44	16.03	1.837	0.295	16.08	812.55	86.10
$MU_{11} \times NB_4D_2$	457.88	94.85	522.00	39.71	8870.33	16.11	1.815	0.284	15.66	823.00	87.38
$MU_{30} \times MU_{852}$	475.77	95.36	540.00	40.25	8873.55	16.06	1.807	0.303	16.79	859.44	87.70
$MU_{303} \times MG_{414}$	477.11	95.14	536.66	39.54	8634.00	15.87	1.837	0.297	16.15	825.22	85.17
$MU_{303} \times MG_{408}$	482.66	94.17	538.00	40.83	8739.44	15.91	1.817	0.294	16.15	825.44	86.30
$MU_{303} \times NB_4D_2$	458.11	92.03	540.00	39.25	8905.33	15.68	1.759	0.292	16.63	846.22	87.40
$PM \times MU_{852}$	454.77	89.85	540.66	39.26	8483.77	15.08	1.776	0.296	16.67	861.77	83.67

(Contd...)

1	2	3	4	5	6	7	8	9	10	11	12
PM $\times$ MG_{414}	380.55	94.88	535.33	40.30	8389.66	15.28	1.821	0.297	16.34	844.66	82.86
PM $\times$ MG_{408}	445.44	94.67	540.00	39.28	8308.89	15.09	1.823	0.285	15.63	819.22	81.90
PM $\times$ NB_4D_2	390.00	94.74	544.00	39.28	8783.06	15.74	1.788	0.290	16.23	854.77	86.68
Mean	459.24	94.33	545.50	39.77	8681.62	15.79	1.817	0.295	16.28	837.06	85.61

Table 2.3: Analysis of Variance for Parental Races and Hybrids for Eleven Economic Characters

Source of variation	df	Mean sum of Squares										
		Fecudity	Hatching percentage	Larval duration	Larval weight	Cocoon yield by number	Cocoon yield by weight	Cocoon weight	Shell weight	Shell ratio	Filament length	Pupation rate
1	2	3	4	5	6	7	8.	9	10	11	12	13
Replications	2	482.25 NS	2.55 NS	1.48 NS	0.24 NS	14841. 34 NS	0.012 NS	2.2 1 NS	0.11 NS	0.09 NS	665.13 NS	0.25 NS
Treatments	23	5116.78**	10.30 **	2216.71 **	48.36**	144843.04**	15.53 **	1751.06**	67.73**	3.93 **	53285.01**	16.42**
Parents	7	7624.13**	20.03 **	3695.87**	150.33**	133134.92**	5.68 **	2177.81**	155.57**	11.34**	162010.64**	6.79 **
Crosses	15	2959.31**	6.44**	422.45**	1.02*	92315.00**	0.40 **	32.00**	2.01**	0.50**	1559.22**	8.77 **
Parent v/s crosses	1	19927.31**	0.268 NS	18776.53**	44.60**	1014720.44**	146.51**	24549.66**	438.55**	3.57**	68092.28**	198.54**
Error	46	603.39	0.44	13.40	0.44	5644.15	0.02	2.61	0.09 0.04	238.38	0.55	

** : Significant ($P<0.01$)

* : Significant ($P<0.05$)

NS : Non-Significant

Table 2.4: General Combining Ability Effects of Eight Parental Races for Eleven Economic Characters

	Fecundity	Hatching percentage	Larval duration	Larval weight	Cocoon yield by number	Cocoon yield by weight	Cocoon weight	Shell weight	Shell ratio	Filament length	Pupation rate
	1	2	3	4	5	6	7	8	9	10	11
Lines											
MU_1	11.19	0.47	-3.31**	0.17	8.91	0.22**	2.37**	0.41**	0.01	0.04	0.16
MU_{11}	16.19	0.47	-6.34**	-0.11^{NS}	72.00**	0.16**	0.33	-0.09 ^{NS}	-0.07 ^{NS}	-13.65 ^{NS}	0.65
MU_{303}	14.16	-0.1 5^{NS}	0.66^{NS}	0.19	106.50**	0.08	-1.28	0.06	0.14	2.79**	1.02
PM	-41.55**	-0.79^{NS}	8.99^{NS}	-0.24^{NS}	-187.41**	-0.46 ^{NS}	-1.42 ^{NS}	-0.38 ^{NS}	-0.07 ^{NS}	10.81**	-1.831*
Testerst											
MU_{852}	12.91	-0.9^{NS}	-5.50**	0.12	21.16	0.04	-0.10 ^{NS}	0.96**	0.51**	26.31**	0.18
MG_{414}	-4.77^{NS}	0.80**	5.35 ^{NS}	-0.17^{NS}	-81.91^{NS}	-0.05^{NS}	1.11	0.16	-0.01 ^{NS}	-7.45^{NS}	-0.77^{NS}
MG_{408}	11.66	0.15	11.99 ^{NS}	0.27	-107.66^{NS}	-0.09^{NS}	1.13	-0.44^{NS}	-0.34 ^{NS}	-2 1.29^{NS}	-1.00^{NS}
NB_4D_2	-19.80^{NS}	-0.04^{NS}	-11.87**	-0.22^{NS}	-68.41**	0.10	2.25**	-0.68^{NS}	-0.16 ^{NS}	2.43**	1.59
S.E	11.70	0.26	1.55	0.30	25.03	0.06	0.68	0.11	0.08	0.25	2.36

** : Significant ($P<0.01$); * : Significant ($P<0.05$); NS : Non-Significant

Table 2.5: Specific Combining Ability of Sixteen Multi Bihybxids for Eleven Economic Characters

Hybrids	Fecundity	Hatching percentage	Larval duration	Larval weight	Cocoon yield by number	Cocoon yield by weight	Cocoon weight	Shell weight	Shell ratio	Filament length	Pupation rate
1	2	3	4	5	6	7	8	9	10	11	12
$MU_1 \times MU_{852}$	7.36	0.15*	-2.64	0.26	36.00	0.44**	5.92**	0.86**	0.07	8.12**	0.43
$MU_1 \times MG_{414}$	14.88	0.61*	-2.77	0.35	115.08**	0.13	4.05**	0.24*	0.23*	9.31**	1.07
$MU_1 \times MG_{408}$	-8.66^{NS}	0.01	-1.81	-0.34^{NS}	-49.49^{NS}	-0.25^{NS}	-1.90^{NS}	-0.29 ns	0.03	15.06**	-0.63^{NS}
$MU_1 \times NB_4D_2$	11.13	0.75*	-1.68	0.24	-29.58^{NS}	-0.05^{NS}	0,04	-0.32 ns	-0.16^{NS}	-13.87^{NS}	-0.05^{NS}
$MU_{11} \times MU_{852}$	6.25	0.82*	-1.66	0.51	3.24	0.30*	3.43*	0.05	0.28*	13.48**	0.13
$MU_{11} \times MG_{414}$	9.00	-0.08^{NS}	2.14^{NS}	-1.05^{NS}	-20.00^{NS}	0.08	1.41*	0.04	-0. 11^{NS}	6.70**	-0.23^{NS}
$MU_{11} \times MG_{408}$	-4.99^{NS}	-0.83^{NS}	4.84^{NS}	0.26	68.41*	0.16*	0.40	0.42*	0.21*	-20.12^{NS}	0.84
$MU_{11} \times NB_4D_2$	2.25	0.09	-5.32**	0.27	-51.66^{NS}	0.04	1.61*	-0.41 ns	-0.38^{NS}	-0.07^{NS}	-0.47^{NS}
$MU_{303} \times MU_{852}$	10.55	2.09**	-0.66	0.15	64.41*	0.14	0.21	0,27*	0.15	11.95**	0.86
$MU_{303} \times MG_{414}$	8.47	0.15*	-4.85**	-0.25^{NS}	-72.16*3	0.04	2.06*	-0.15NS	-0.26^{NS}	-4.40^{NS}	-0.69^{NS}
$MU_{303} \times MG_{408}$	-2.41^{NS}	-0.15^{NS}	-0.16	0.59	58.91*	0.12	0.08	0.16	0.06	9.65**	0.66

(Contd...)

1	2	3	4	5	6	7	8	9	10	11	12
$MU_{303} \times NB_4D_2$	4.50	-2.09 NS	5.67 NS	-0.49 NS	-51.16 NS	-0.30N NS	-2.36 NS	0.26*	0.35**	6.70**	0.83
$PM \times MU_{852}$	24.16*	-2.77 NS	-0.32	-0.40 NS	-31.66 NS	-0.28 NS	-2.70 NS	-0.53"3	-0.05 NS	-9.65 NS	-0.29 NS
$PM \times MG_{414}$	-32.36 NS	0.54*	5.47 NS	0.94*	-22.91 NS	0.01	0.57	0.35*	0.14	7.01**	-0.14 NS
$PM \times MG_{408}$	16.08	0.97*	-6.49**	-0.51 NS	-77.83 NS	-0.03 NS	1.42*	-0.29 ns	-0.28 NS	-4.59 NS	-0.86 NS
$PM \times NB_4D_2$	-7.88 NS	1.25*	1.34 NS	-0.02 NS	132.41**	0.31*	0.70	0.47*	0.18*	7.23**	1.30
S.E	23.40	0.53	3.11	0.61	50.07	0.12	1.36	0.23	0.16	0.51	4.73

** : Significant (P<0.01)

* : Significant (P<0.05)

NS : Non-Significant.

Table 2.6: Analysis of Variance for Combining Ability for Eleven Economic Characters

Source of variation	df	Mean sum of squares										
		Fecundity	Hatching percentage	Larval duration	Larval weight	Cocoon yield by number	Cocoon yield by weight	Cocoon weight	Shell weight	Shell ratio	Filament length	Pupation rate
Replications	2	1169.18^{NS}	2.13^{NS}	1.00*5	0.43	19602.33^{NS}	0.40^{NS}	0.60^{NS}	0.33^{NS}	0.16^{NS}	1.80^{NS}	813.98^{NS}
Crosses	15	2959.31**	6.44**	422.45**	1.02	92315.00**	0.40**	32.00**	2.01**	0.50**	8.77**	1559.22**
Line	3	9260.60**	4.42^{NS}	529.93**	0.56	2069231.05**	1.20**	37.71**	1.33**	0.13^{NS}	19.51**	1245. 00^{NS}
Tester	3	2872. 10^{NS}	6.04^{NS}	1372.06**	0.67	188458.61**	0.09^{NS}	30.37**	6.46**	1.63**	16.68**	4830.34**
Line × Tester	9	887.96^{NS}	7.24**	70.09**	1.29*	22064.14**	0.24**	30.63**	0.75**	0.24**	2.56**	573.59^{NS}
Error	30	821.54	0.43	14.54	0.57	3762.00	0.02	2.80	0.08	0.04	0.403	333.56

** : Significant ($P<0.01$)

* : Significant ($P < 0.05$)

NS : Non-Significant.

Table 2.7: Estimates of Heterosis for Eleven Economic Characters

Hybrids	Fecundity percentage	Hatching duration	Larval weight	Larval yield by number	Cocoon yield by weight	Cocoon weight	Cocoon weight	Shell ratio	Shell length	Filament rate	Pupation
1	2	3	4	5	6	7	8	9	10	11	12
MU_1× MU_{852}	-5.94^{NS}	-1.17^{NS}	-4.68**	1.16**	-3.49^{NS}	28.10**	32.47**	29.26**	-0.59**	11.00**	-4.64^{NS}
MU_1× MG_{414}	-4.40^{NS}	0.02	-3.85*	2.84**	-3.98^{NS}	20.76**	25.81**	21.05**	-2.43^{NS}	3.80**	-4.14^{NS}
MU_1× MG_{408}	-4.54^{NS}	0.32	-1.78	2.81**	-5.40^{NS}	19.34**	25.61**	17.67**	4.88**	5.51**	-6.45^{NS}
MU_1× NB_4D_2	9.67	1.11*	-6.78**	2.35**	-1.20^{NS}	24.09**	25.86**	18.36**	4.25**	6.02**	-2.58^{NS}
MU_{11}× MU_{852}	-5.72^{NS}	-1.06^{NS}	-5.58**	2.62**	2.16	23.14**	24.52**	23.57**	0.88**	8.60**	-3.54^{NS}
MU_{11}× MG_{414}	-5.58^{NS}	-0.36^{NS}	-3.12*	-1.28NS	4.46	22.52**	27.90**	20.24**	4.62**	2.85**	-5.31^{NS}
MU_{11}× MG_{408}	-3.82^{NS}	- 1 .48^{NS}	-1.37	3.82**	3.07	22.45**	25.82**	18.47**	4,34**	3.26**	-4.05^{NS}
MU_{11}× NB_4D_2	9.40	-0.53^{NS}	-7.58**	1.89**	-0.41^{NS}	24.78**	25.51**	15.91**	6.22**	3.36**	-2.33^{NS}
MU_{303}× MU_{852}	-6.86^{NS}	0.29	-5.06**	2.80**	-0.94^{NS}	25.07**	25.74**	21.68**	1.69**	7.01**	-1.67^{NS}
MU_{303}× MG_{414}	-5.98^{NS}	-0.07^{NS}	-4.02*	1.82**	4.50	21.51**	27.04**	18.80**	5.50**	3.08**	-5.10^{NS}
MU_{303}× MG_{408}	-3.60^{NS}	-0.75^{NS}	-1.95	5.80**	2.63	21.54**	24.28**	16.66**	5.16**	3.46**	-3.51^{NS}
MU_{303}× NB_4D_2	9.26	-2.81^{NS}	-5.28**	1.00*	-0.14^{NS}	21.45**	21.47**	17.74**	1.71**	5.83**	-1.98^{NS}

(Contd...)

1	2	3	4	5	6	7	8	9	10	11	12
PM × MU_{852}	-3.07^{NS}	-1.87^{NS}	-11.29**	9.57**	3.20	27.36**	31.45**	29.25**	1.39**	24.06**	-4.32^{NS}
PM × MG_{414}	8.31*	3.46**	-8.71**	13.48**	5.17	26.69**	33.89**	29.13**	-0.66^{NS}	20.75**	-5.85^{NS}
PM × MG_{408}	-2.97^{NS}	3.60**	-9.49**	11.36**	5.39	24.81**	32.48**	23.37**	4.63**	17.57**	-6.60^{NS}
PM × NB_4D_2	15.81	3.89**	-12.23**	10.52**	-0.96^{NS}	32.15**	31.27**	27.19**	-0.30^{NS}	22.36**	-0.85^{NS}
S.E	17.36	0.47	2,58	0.47	53.12	0.11	1.14	0.22	0.14	0.52	10.91

** : Significant (P<0.01)

* : Significant (P<0.05)

NS : Non-Significant.

Table 2.8: Estimates of Over-dominance for Eleven Economic Characters

Hybrids	Fecundity	Hatching Percentage	Larval duration	Larval weight	Cocoon yield by number	Cocoon yield by weight	Cocoon weight	Shell weight	Shell ratio	Filament length	Pupation rate
1	2	3	4	5	6	7	8	9	10	11	12
$MU_1 \times MU_{852}$	-12.50^{NS}	1.49**	-3.57**	11.47**	5.71**	13.79**	15.21**	3.24**	10.24**	10.69**	-6.03^{NS}
$MU_1 \times MG_{414}$	-10.56^{NS}	-0.45^{NS}	-2.60**	9.43**	5.32**	5.89**	8.63**	-3.85^{NS}	11.49**	16.79**	-5.43^{NS}
$MU_1 \times MG_{408}$	-9.60^{NS}	0.18	0.59^{NS}	9.05**	7.39**	4.39**	7.88**	-6.98^{NS}	13.90**	15.24**	-7.76^{NS}
$MU_1 \times NB_4D_2$	-15.09^{NS}	1.03*	-5.48**	9.91**	4.17**	9.69**	8.85**	-5.22^{NS}	12.82**	14.95**	-4.02^{NS}
$MU_{11} \times MU_{852}$	-11.37^{NS}	1.66**	-4.08**	10.38**	4.12**	8.10**	8.30**	-1.29^{NS}	8.79**	11.54**	-4.72^{NS}
$MU_{11} \times MG_{414}$	- 10.73^{NS}	-0.83^{NS}	-1.44	13.26**	5.50**	7.02**	10.73**	-4.50^{NS}	13.77**	16.55**	-5.89^{NS}
$MU_{11} \times MG_{408}$	-7.95^{NS}	2.27**	0.24^{NS}	8.34**	4.81**	6.79**	8.05**	-6,34^{NS}	13.31**	16.84**	-4.96^{NS}
$MU_{11} \times NB_4D_2$	-13.95^{NS}	1.52**	-5.88**	10.52**	3.11**	9.96**	8.55**	-7.18^{NS}	14.51**	16.07**	-3.55^{NS}
$MU_{303} \times MU_{852}$	- 12.54^{NS}	0.21	-4.48**	10.49**	2.76**	10.75**	9.51**	-1.62^{NS}	9.97**	12.47**	-2.55^{NS}
$MU_{303} \times MG_{414}$	- 11.20^{NS}	-0.30^{NS}	-3.30*	10.78**	5.38**	6.22**	10.13**	-4.50^{NS}	13.45**	16.01**	-5.36^{NS}
$MU_{303} \times MG_{408}$	7.84**	-0.87^{NS}	-1.29*	6.88**	4.23**	5.99**	6.88**	-6.66^{NS}	12.93**	15.52**	-4.11^{NS}
$MU_{303} \times NB_4D_2$	-13.90^{NS}	3.12**	-4.48**	11.55**	2.41**	7.03**	5.20**	-4.57^{NS}	9.22**	13.70**	-2.88^{NS}
$PM \times MU_{852}$	-16.4Q^{NS}	5.58**	-4.13**	12.69**	3.48**	4.00**	7.63**	-3.89^{NS}	10.61**	11.41**	-5.33^{NS}

(Contd...)

1	2	3	4	5	6	7	8	9	10	11	12
PM × MG_{414}	-29.17^{NS}	-0.57^{NS}	-1.22**	9.07**	6.33**	2.27**	9.17**	-4. 50^{NS}	12.43**	14.03**	-7.41^{NS}
PM × MG_{408}	-14.95^{NS}	-0.12^{NS}	-2.15**	10.42**	5.86**	1.26**	7.23**	-9.23^{NS}	5.74**	16.15**	-7.85^{NS}
PM × NB_4D_2	-26.70^{NS}	0.34	-4.94**	11.49**	0.64**	7.44**	6.93**	5.22**	11 .40**	12.83**	-1.89^{NS}
S.E	6.24	0.54	2.98	0.54	1.34	0.12	1.32	0.25	0.17	0.60	12.60

** : Significant ($P<0.01$)

* : Significant ($P<0.05$)

NS : Non-Significant

The details pertaining to the mean performance of the parents and the hybrids as well as the general combining ability of the parents and specific combining ability of the hybrids and the degree of manifestation of heterosis and over dominance for each one of the eleven economic traits analyzed are presented.

Fecundity

The fecundity was observed to be much higher in all the three multivoltine parental races with the range of values from 468.22 (MU_1) to 478.77 (MU_{11}) compared to control Pure Mysore (394.44). Similarly, the fecundity of the three bivoltine parental races was found to be marginally better with a range of 532.77 in MG_{408} to 544 in MG_{852} than the control NB_4D_2 (532.11) (Table 2.1). On the other hand, the fecundity in all the hybrids even though was found to be higher with range of values from 380.55 (PM × MG_{414}) to 482.66 (MU_{303} × MG_{408}) than the control hybrid PM × NB_4D_2 (390.00), the values were observed to be lower than the better parents (Table 2.2).

The analysis of variance computed for this trait revealed highly significant variation ($P < 0.01$) for treatments, parents, crosses and parents, with crosses (Table 2.3).

The estimates of general combining ability presented in Table 2.4 revealed variability in multivoltine lines varying from 11.19 (MU_1) to 41.55 (PM), while in bivoltine testers, the estimates were observed to vary from –19.80 (NB_4D_2) to 12.91 (MU_{852}). Interestingly control Pure Mysore was observed to be a good general combiner followed by MU_1, MU_{11}, MU_{303} among multivoltine lines. On the other hand MU_{852} and MG_{303} were shown to be average general combiners and MG_{414} and NB_4D_2 as poor general combiners among bivoltine testers (Table 2.4).

The specific combining ability effects estimated for sixteen hybrids recorded in Table 2.5 were found to vary from -32.36 (PM × MG_{414}) to 24.16 (PM × MU_{852}). Out of sixteen hybrids eleven hybrids were found to express positive values for this trait.

The analysis of variance computed for the combining ability was found to reveal highly significant variations ($P < 0.01$) for crosses and line. While, non-significant ($P > 0.01$) for tester and Line × Tester (Table 2.6).

The heterosis values were found to vary from -6.86 (MU_{303} × MU_{852}) to 9.67 in MU_1× NB_4D_2 but higher in PM × NB_4D_2 15.81 (PM × MG_{414}). The heterotic effect was found to be positive in live hybrids, out of which, PM × MG_{414} in was found to excel the other hybrids (Table 2.7). On the other hand the over dominance effect was observed in only one hybrid MU_{303} X MG_{408}. While it was found to vary from -29.17 (PM X MG_{414}) to 7.84 in M_{303} X MG_{408} (Table 2.8).

Hatching Percentage

The hatching percentage was observed to be much higher in all the three multivoltine races with a range of values from 94.54% (MU_1) to 96.32% (MU_{11}) compared to control Pure Mysore (87.98). Similarly, the hatching percentage of the three bivoltine parental races was found to be marginally better with a range of 94.43% (MG_{414}) to 95.16% MU_{852}) than the control NB_4D_2 (94.41%) (Table 2.1 and 2.2). Among the hybrids, the hatching percentage was found to vary from 89.85% (PM X MU_{852}) to 95. 52% (MU_1× NB_4D_2 and MU_{11} × MG_{414}). Out of fifteen new hybrids studied, only seven hybrids were found to be superior then the control hybrid, PM × NB_4D_2 (94.74%) (Table 2.3).

The analysis of variance computed for this trait revealed highly significant variations ($P<0.01$) for treatments, parents, crosses, while non-significant variation ($P > 0.01$) for parent with crosses (Table 2.3).

The estimates of general combining ability presented in Table 2.4 revealed the variability ranging from -0.78 PM to 0.47 (MU_1 and MU_{11}) among lines, while from -0.91 (MU_{852}) to 0.80 (MG_{414}) among testers. The tester MG_{414} was observed to be a good general combiner, While MU_1, MU_{11} among multivoltine lines and MG_{408} among bivoltine tester were found to be average general combiners. On the other hand the remaining parental races were found to be poor general combiners.

The specific combining ability effects estimated for sixteen hybrids recorded in Table 2.2 were found to vary from -2.77 (PM × MU_{852}) to 2.09 (MU_{303} × MU_{852}). Out of sixteen hybrids, eleven hybrids were found to express positive values for this trait, out of which only one hybrid MU_{303} X MU_{852} was found to be a good specific combiner, eight hybrids as average specific combiners and the remaining hybrids were observed to be poor combiners.

The analysis of variance computed for the combining ability was found to reveal highly significant variation ($P < 0.01$) for crosses and line × tester, while non-significant variation ($P > 0.01$) for line and tester (Table 2.6).

The heterosis for this trait was found to vary from -2.81 (MU_{303} × NB_4D_2) to 3.89 (PM × NB_4D_2). The heterotic effect was found to be positive in seven hybrids. Out of which, three hybrids viz., PM × MG_{414}, PM × NB_4D_2, PM× MG_{408} were found to excel the other hybrids (Table 2.7). On the other hand, the over dominance effect was found to vary from -0.87 (MU_{303} × MG_{408}) to 5.58 (PM × MU_{852}). Out of sixteen hybrids, nine hybrids were found to have positive values for this trait (Table 2.8).

Larval Duration

The value prefixed with negative sign for this trait were considered as desirable because reduced larval duration is of economic importance. All the three multivoitine parental races was found to register shorter larval duration with a range of values from 559.33 h (MU_{11}) to 554.66 h (MU_{11})

compared to control PM (664.66 h). Similarly, all the three bivoltine parental races with a range of values 573.88 h (MG_{414}) to 572.53 h (MU_{852}) were found to excel the control NB_4D_2 (575 hrs) marginally (Table 2.1). While all the fifteen new hybrids were found to register shorter larval duration with a range of 540.66 h (PM × MU_{852}) to 522 hrs (MU_{11} × NB_4D_2) than the control hybrid PM × NB_4D_2 (544 h) (Table 2.2).

The analysis of variance computed for this trait revealed highly significant values (P<0.01) for all the sources of variation (Table 2.3).

The estimates of general combining ability presented in Table 2.4 revealed that the values vary in multivoltine lines from 8.99(PM) to –6.34 (MU_{11}) while in bivoltine testers from 11.99 (MG_{408}) to –11.87 (NB_4D_2). Among them MU_1 and MU_{11} were observed to be the good general combiners along with two bivoltine testers MG_{414} and NB_4D_2. While the remaining lines and testers were found to be poor general combiners (Table 2.4).

The specific combining ability effects estimated for sixteen hybrids recorded in Table 2.5 were found to vary from 5.67 (MU_{303} × NB_4D_2) to –6.49 (PM × MG_{408}). Out of sixteen hybrids, eleven hybrids were found to express negative specific combining ability effects (considered as positive for this trait). Out of which three hybrids MU_{11} × NB_4D_2, MU_{303} × MG_{414} and PM × MG_{408} were found to be a good specific combiners (Table 2.5).

The analysis of variance computed for the combining ability was found to reveal highly significant values (P<0.01) for all the sources of variation except for replication (Table 2.6).

The heterosis for this trait was found to vary from –1.37 in MU_1 × MG_{408} to –11.29 in PM × MU_{852}. All the hybrids expressed negative values (considered as positive heterosis) positive values, out of which ten hybrids were found to reveal highly significant (P<0.01) heterotic effect (Table 2.7). Similarly the over dominance effect was found to vary from 0.59 (MU_{11} × MG_{408}) to –5.88 (MU_{11} × NB_4D_2). Out of sixteen, fourteen hybrids reveal positive values out of which seven hybrids were found to express highly (P<0.01) significant over dominance effect for this trait (Table 2.8).

Larval Weight

Larval weight was observed to be much higher in all the three multivoltinc parental races with a range of values from 33.34 grams (MU_{303})to 33.74 grams (MU_1) compared to control Pure Mysore (26.70). Similarly, the larval weight of the three bivoltine parental races was found to be marginally better with a range of 44.33 gram (MG_{414}) to 44.97 (MU_{852}) than the control NB_4D_2 (43.38 gram) (Table 2.1). On the other hand, of the fifteen new hybrids studied, eleven hybrids were found to be superior with a range of 38.44 grams (MU_{11}× MG_{414}) to 40.83 (MU_{303}× MG_{408}) than the control PM × NB_4D_2 (39.28 gram) (Table 2.2).

The analysis of variance computed for this trait revealed highly significant variation (P<0.01) for treatments, parents and parents vs. crosses, while significant variation (P<0.05) for crosses (Table 2.3).

The estimate of general combining ability presented in Table 2.4 revealed the variability ranging from –0.24 (PM) top 0.17 (MU_1) among multivoltine lines, while from –0.22 (NB_4D_2) to 0.12 (MU_{852}) among bivoltine testers. The multivoltine lines MU_1, MU_{303} and the bivoltine testers MU_{852}, MG_{408} were found to be average general combiners, while the remaining parental races were found to be poor general combiners.

The sca effects estimated for sixteen hybrids recorded in Table 2.5 was found to vary from –1.05 (MU_{11}× MG_{414}) to 0.95 (PM × MG_{414}). Out of sixteen hybrids, nine hybrids were found to express positive values for this trait out of which only one hybrid (PM × MG_{414}) was found to be good specific combiner, while eight hybrids were found to be average specific combiners and the remaining hybrids are poor specific combiners.

The analysis of variance computed for the combining ability was found to reveal significant ($P<0.05$) variation for Line x Tester, while non-significant ($P>0.05$) variation among crosses, line and tester (Table 2.6).

The heterosis for this trait was found to vary from –1.28 (MU_1 × MG_{414}) to 13.48 (PM × MG_{414}). Out of sixteen hybrids, fourteen hybrids were found to be positive having highly significant heterotic effect, out of which four hybrids PM × MU_{852}, PM × MG_{414}, PM × MG_{408}, PM × NB_4D_2 were found to excel the other hybrids (Table 2.7). On the other hand, all the hybrids were found to be highly significant with a range of values from 6.88 (MU_{303} × MG_{408}) to 13.26 (MU_{11} × MG_{414}) for over dominance effect of which the hybrids MU_1 MU_{852}, MU_{11} × $MG_{414,}$ MU_{303} × NB_4D_2, MU_{303} × NB_4D_2, PM × MG_{408} were found to excel the other hybrids (Table 2.8).

Cocoon Yield by Number

The cocoon yield by number was observed to be much higher in all the three new multivoltine parental races with a range of 9125.66 (MU_{303}) to 9214.31(MU_1) compared to control PM (8739.11). Similarly, all the three bivoltine parental races were found to be much higher with a range of values from 8790 (MU_{852}) to 8956.66 (MG_{414}) than the control NB_4D_2 (8659.10) (Table 2.1). On the other hand, of the fifteen new hybrids studied, only four hybrids MU_1 × NB_4D_2, MU_{11} × NB_4D_2, MU_{303}× MU_{852} and MU_{303}× NB_4D_2 were found to be superior with a range of values from 8389.66 (PM × MG_{414}) to 8905.33 (MU_{303} × NB_4D_2 than the control PM × NB_4D_2 (8783.06) (Table 2.2).

The analysis of variance computed for this trait revealed highly significant values (P<0.01) for all the sources of variation except for replications (Table 2.3).

The estimates of general combining ability presented in Table 2.4 revealed the variability ranging from 8.91 (MU_1) to –187.41 among multivoltine parental races, while from –107.66 (MG_{408}) to 168.41 (NB_4D_2) among bivoltine testers. The multivoltine lines MU_1, $MU_{11,}$ and MU_{303} and the bivoltine testers NB_4D_2 were found to be good general combiners followed by the line MU_1 and the tester MU_{852} which were found to be average general combiners, while the remaining parental races were found to be poor general combiners.

The specific combining ability effects estimated for sixteen hybrids recorded in Table 2.5 were found to vary from –77.83 (PM × MG_{408}) to 132.41 (PM × NB_4D_2). Of the sixteen hybrids, seven were found to express positive values for this trait, out of which two hybrids MU_1 × MG_{414} and PM ´ NB_4D_2 were found to be good specific combiners followed by the hybrids, MU_{11} × MG_{408},MU_{303} × MU_{852} and MU_{303} × MU_{408} which were observed to be average specific combiners, while the remaining hybrids were found to be poor specific combiners.

The analysis of variance computed for combining ability was found to reveal highly significant values (P<0.01) for all the sources of variation except for replications (Table 2.6).

The estimate of heterosis for this trait was found to, vary from –5.40 (MU_1 × MG_{408}) to 5.39 (PM × MG_{408}). Out of sixteen hybrids, eight were found to be having positive values of which four hybrids MU_{11} × MG_{414}, MU_{303} ´ MG_{414}, PM × MG_{414} and PM × MG_{408} were found to excel the other hybrids. (Table 2.7). On the otherhand, all the hybrids were found to be highly significant (p<0.01) with a range of 0.64 (PM × NB_4D_2) to 7.39 (MU_1 × MU_{408}) for over dominance effect. Of which seven hybrids, MU_1 MU_{852}, MU_1 MU_{414}, $MU_1 \times MG_{408}$, $MU_{11} \times MG_{414}$, $MU_{303} \times MG_{414}$, PM × MG_{414} and PM × MG_{408} were found to excel the other hybrids (Table 2.8).

Cocoon Yield by Weight

Cocoon yield by weight was observed to be much higher in all the three multivoltine parental races with a range of values from 11.17 kg (MU_1) to 11.26 kgs (MU_1) compared to control Pure Mysore (9.17 kg). Similarly, cocoon yield by weight of the three bivoltine parental races were found to be marginally better with a range of 14.66Kgs (MU_{852}) to 15.01 kgs (MG_{408}) than the control NB_4D_2 (14.65 kgs) (Table 2.1). On the other hand, of the fifteen new hybrids studied, ten hybrids were found to be marginally superior with a range of 15.08 kgs (PM × MU_{852}) to 16.50 kgs ($MU_1 \times MU_{852}$) than the control hybrid PM × NB_4D_2 (15.74 kg) (Table 2.2).

The analysis of variance computed for this trait revealed highly significant values ($P<0.01$) for all the sources of variation except for replication (Table 2.3).

The general combining ability effect estimated for this trait revealed the variability ranging from –0.46 (PM) to 0.22 (MU_1) among multivoltine lines and from –0.09 (MG_{408}) to 0.10 (NB_4D_2) among bivoltine testers. The multivoltine lines MU_1 and MU_{11} were found to be good general combiners, followed MU_{303}. The bivoltine testers MU_{852}, NB_4D_2 were found to be average general combiners, While, the remaining parental races were found to be poor general combiners (Table 2.4).

The specific combining ability effect estimated for sixteen hybrids revealed the variability from –0.30 (MU_{303} $\times NB_4D_2$) to 0.44 ($MU_1 \times MU_{852}$). Out of sixteen hybrids, eleven hybrids were found to express positive specific combining ability effects, out of which only one hybrid MU_1 ´ MU_{852} was found to be a good specific combiner, followed by three hybrids. $MU_{11} \times MU_{852}$, $MU_{11} \times MG_{408}$ and PM× NB_4D_2 as average specific combiners. While, the remaining hybrids were found to be poor specific combiners (Table 2.5).

The analysis of variance computed for the combining ability was found to reveal highly significant variations (P<0.01) for crosses, Line, Line × Tester, While, non-significant variation (P>0.01) for tester (Table 2.6).

The heterosis recorded for this trait was found to vary from 19.34 ($MU_1 \times MG_{408}$) to 32.15 (PM × NB_4D_2). All the sixteen hybrids were found to express positive and highly significant (P<0.01) values. Of which, the hybrids $MU_1 \times MU_{852}$, $MU_{303} \times MU_{852}$, PM × MU_{852}, PM × MG_{414} and PM× NB_4D_2 were found to excel the other hybrids (Table 2.7). On the other hand, all the sixteen hybrids were found to express highly significant over-dominance effect with a range of 1.26 (PM × MG_{408}) to 13.79 ($MU_1 \times MU_{852}$). Of which, the four hybrids $MU_1 \times MU_{852}$, MU_1, × NB_4D_2, $MU_{11} \times NB_4D_2$ and $MU_{303} \times MU_{852}$ were found to excel the other hybrids for this trait (Table 2.8).

Cocoon Weight

Cocoon weight was observed to be much higher in all the three multivoltine parental races with a range of values from 1.220 g (MU_{11}) to 1.225 g (MU_1, MU_{11} and MU_{303}) compared to control Pure Mysore (1.053 g). Similarly, the cocoon weight of the three bivoltine parental races was found to be marginally better with a range of 1.681 g (MU_{852}) to 1.701 g (MG_{408}) than the control NB_4D_2 (1.672 g) (Table 2.1). Of the fifteen new hybrids studied, thirteen hybrids were found to be superior with a range of 1.759 g ($MU_{303} \times NB_4D_2$) to 1.90 gm ($MU_1 \times MU_{852}$) than the control hybrid PM × NB_4D_2 (1.78 g) (Table 2.2).

The analysis of variance computed for this trait revealed highly significant values (P<0.01) for all the sources of variations (Table 2.3).

The estimates of general combining ability presented in Table 2.4 revealed the variability from –1.42 (PM) to 2.37 (MU_1) among multivoltine lines and from –0.10 (MU_{852}) to 2.25 (NB_4D_2) among bivoltine testers. The multivoltine lines MU_1 and the bivoltine tester NB_4D_2 were found to be good general combiners, followed by the lines MU_{11}, MU_{303} and the testers MG_{414}, MG_{408} as average general combiners, While, the remaining parental races were found to be poor general combiners.

The specific combining ability effects estimated for sixteen hybrids was found to reveal variability from –2.70 (PM × MU_{852}) to 5.92 (MU_1 × MU_{852}). Of the sixteen hybrids, thirteen hybrids were found to express positive values for this trait, out of which two hybrids MU_1× MU_{852} and MU_1× MG_{414} were found to be good specific combiners followed by four hybrids of MU_{11} × MU_{852}, MU_{11}× MG_{414}, MU_{11},× NB_4D_2, PM × MG_{408} as average specific combiners, while, the remaining hybrids were found to be poor specific combiners (Table 2.5).

The analysis of variance computed for the combining ability was found to reveal highly significant values ($P<0.01$) for all the sources of variation (Table 2.6).

The heterosis for this trait was found to vary from 21.47 (MU_{303}× NB_4D_2) to 33.89 (PM × MG_{414}). All the sixteen hybrids were found to reveal highly significant value, of which, five hybrids, MU_1 × MU_{852}, PM × MU_{852}, PM × MG_{414}, PM × MG_{408} and PM × NB_4D_2 were found to excel the others. (Table 2.7). On the other hand, all the sixteen hybrids were found to exhibit highly significant values for over dominance ranging from 5.20 (MU_{303}× NB_4D_2) to 15.21 (MU_1 × MU_{852}). The four hybrids MU_1× MU_{852}, MU_{303} × MU_{852}, MU_{303} × MG_{414} and PM × MG_{414} were found to excel the other hybrids for this trait (Table 2.8).

Shell Weight

Shell weight was observed to be much higher in all. the three multivoltine parental races with a range of values from 0.184 g (MU_1) to 0.190 g (MU_{303}) compared to control Pure Mysore (0.150 g). Similarly, the shell weight of the three bivoltine parental races were found to be marginally better with a range of 0.307 g (MU_{852}) to 0.314 g (MG_{408}) than the control NB_4D_2 (0.306 g) (Table 2.1). On the other hand, of the fifteen new hybrids studied, thirteen hybrids were found to be superior with a range of 0.285 g (PM × MG_{408}) to 0.318 g (MU_1 × MU_{852}) than the control hybrid PM × NB_4D_2 (0.290 g) (Table 2.2).

The analysis of variance computed for this trait revealed highly significant values (P<0.01) for all the sources of variations (Table 2.3).

The variability recorded for general combining ability estimates from –0.38 (PM) to 0.41 (MU_1) among the multivoltine lines while in bivoltine testers it varies from –0.68 (NB_4D_2) to 0.96 (MU_{852}). The multivoltine line MU_1 and the bivoltine tester MU_{852} were found to be good general combiners followed by the line MU_{303} and the tester MG_{414} as average general combiners. While, the remaining parental races were found to be poor general combiners (Table 2.4).

The specific combining ability effects estimated for sixteen hybrids reveal variability from –0.53 (PM × MU_{852}) to 0.86 (MU_1 × MU_{852}). Out of sixteen hybrids, ten hybrids were found to posses positive values for this trait. Of which the hybrid MU_1 × MU_{852} was found to be good specific combiner, followed by the hybrids MU_1 × MG_{414}, MU_{11} × MG_{408}, MU_{303} × MU_{852}, MU_{303} × NB_4D_2, PM × MG_{414} and PM × NB_4D_2 which were observed to be average specific combiners. While, the remaining hybrids who found to be poor specific combiners (Table 2.5).

The analysis of variance computed for the combining ability was found to reveal highly significant values (P<0.01) for all the sources of variations (Table 2.6).

The heterosis estimated for this trail was found to vary from 15.91 (MU_{11} × NB_4D_2) to 29.26 (MU_1 × MU_{852}). The values were found to be highly significant in all the hybrids of which four hybrids MU_1 × MU_{852}, PM × MU_{852}, PM × MG_{414} and PM × NB_4D_2 were found to excel the other hybrids (Table 2.7). On the other hand, the over dominance effect recorded for this trait was found to vary from –9.23 (PM× MG_{408}) to 3.24 (MU_1 × MU_{852}). Only two hybrids MU_1 × MU_{852} and PM × NB_4D_2 were found to be having highly significant values, while the remaining hybrids were found to be having negative and non-significant values for this trait (Table 2.8).

Shell ratio

Shell ratio was observed to be much higher in all the three multivoltine parental races with a range of values from 15.04% to 15.52 (MU_{303}) compared to control Pure Mysore (14.24%). Similarly, the shell ratio of the three bivoltine parental races were found to be marginally better with a range of 18.55% (MG_{408}) to 18.66% (MG_{414}) than the control NB_4D_2 (18.31%) (Table 2.1). On the other hand, of the fifteen new hybrids studied, seven hybrids were found to be superior with a range of values from 15.63% (PM × MG_{408}) to 17.01% (MU_{11} × MU_{852}) than the control hybrid PM × NB_4D_2 (16.23%) (Table 2.2).

The analysis of variance computed for this trait revealed highly significant values (P<0.01) for all the sources of variations (Table 2.3).

The estimates of general combining ability revealed variability, ranging from -0.07 (MU_{11} and PM) to 0.14 (MU_{303}) among multivoltine lines, while they vary from –0.34 (MG_{408}) to 0.51 (MU_{852}) among bivoltine testers. The bivoltine tester MU_{852} was found to be a good general combiner followed by the lines MU_1, and MU_{303}, the remaining parental races were found to be poor general combiners (Table 2.4).

The specific combining ability effects estimated for sixteen hybrids revealed variability from –0.38 ($MU_{11} \times NB_4D_2$) to 0.35 ($MU_{303} \times NB_4D_2$). Out of sixteen hybrids, ten hybrids were found to express positive values for this trait, of which the hybrid $MU_{303} \times NB_4D_2$ was found to be good specific combiner followed by $MU_1 \times MG_{414}$, $MU_{11} \times MU_{852}$, $MU_{11} \times MG_{408}$, PM $\times NB_4D_2$ which were observed to be average specific combiners. While, the remaining hybrids were found to be poor specific combiners (Table 2.5).

The analysis of variance computed for the combining ability was found to reveal highly significant variations ($P<0.01$) for crosses, Tester and Line X Tester. While, non significant variation ($P>0.01$) for line (Table 2.6).

The heterosis for this trait was found to vary from –2.43 ($MU_1 \times MG_{414}$) to 6.22 ($MU_{11} \times NB_4D_2$). Out of sixteen hybrids, thirteen were found to express positive and highly significant values for heterotic effect. Of which three hybrids $MU_{11} \times NB_4D_2$, $MU_{303} \times MG_{414}$ and $MU_{303} \times MG_{408}$ were found to excel the other hybrids (Table 2.7). On the other hand, all the hybrids were found to be highly significant for over dominance effect with a range of values from 5.74 (PM MG_{408}) to 14.51 ($MU_{11} \times NB_4D_2$), of which five hybrids, MU_1 MG_{408}, $MU_{11} \times MG_{414}$, $MU_{11} \times MG_{408}$, $MU_{11} \times NB_4D_2$ and MU_{303} MG_{414} were found to excel the other hybrids (Table 2.8).

Silk Filament Length

Silk filament length was observed to be much higher in all the three mutlivoltine parental races with a range of value from 592.55 mts (MU_1) to 618.55 m (MU_{303}) compared to control Pure Mysore (416.44 m). Similarly all the three bivoltine parental races are found to exhibit marginally better values for this trait with a range form 982.55 m (MG_{414}) to 987.11 m (MG_{408}) than the control NB_4D_2 (980.66 m) (Table 2.1). On the other hand, the values obtained for the new hybrids for this trait varies from 812.55 m ($MU_{11} \times MG_{408}$), to 862.77 m. ($MU_1 \times MU_{852}$). Of which five hybrids viz $MU_1 \times MU_{852}$, $MU_1 \times MG_{414}$, $MU_{11} \times MU_{852}$, $MU_{303} \times MU_{852}$ and PM$\times MU_{852}$ were found to be superior than the control hybrid, PM NB_4D_2 (854.77 mts) (Table 2.2).

The analysis of variance computed for this trait revealed highly significant variations ($P<0.01$) for all the sources of variations (Table 2.3).

The estimates of general combining ability revealed variability for this trait ranging from –13.65 (MU_{11}) to 10.81 (PM) among multivoltine lines and from –21.29 (MG_{408}) 26.31 to (MU_{852}) among bivoltine testers. The multivoltine lines MU_{303}, PM and the bivoltine testers MU_{852}, NB_4D_2 were found to be good general combiners followed by the line MU_1 as average general combiner. While, the remaining parental races were found to be poor general combiners (Table 2.4).

The specific combining ability effect estimated for sixteen hybrids revealed variability ranging from -20.12 ($MU_{11} \times MG_{408}$) to 15.06 ($MU_1 \times MG_{408}$). Out of sixteen hybrids, ten hybrids were found to be having positive values for this trait, out of which, the hybrids $MU_1 \times MG_{408}$, $MU_{11} \times MU_{852}$ and $MU_{303} \times MU_{852}$ were found to be good specific combiners followed by the hybrids $MU_1 \times MU_{852}$, $MU_1 \times MG_{414}$, $MU_{11} \times MG_{414}$, $MU_{303} \times MG_{408}$, $MU_{303} \times NB_4D_2$, PM $\times MG_{414}$, PM $\times NB_4D_2$ as average general combiners while, the remaining hybrids were found to be poor specific combiners (Table 2.5).

The analysis of variance computed for the combining ability was found to reveal highly significant variations ($P<0.01$) for ail the sources of variations (Table 2.6).

The heterosis estimated for this trait was found to vary from 2.85 ($MU_{11} \times MG_{414}$) to 24.06 (PM $\times MU_{852}$). All the sixteen hybrids were found to express positive and highly significant values, of which the hybrids $MU_1 \times MU_{852}$, PM $\times$ MU_{852}, PM $\times$ MG_{414}, PM $\times$ MG_{408} and PM $\times$ NB_4D_2 were found to excel the others. (Table 2.7). On the other hand, all the sixteen hybrids reveal positive and highly significant over dominance effect with a range of values from 10.69 ($MU_1 \times$ MU_{852}) to 16.84 ($MU_{11} \times MG_{408}$). Of which, eight hybrids MU_1 $\times MG_{414}$, $MU_1 \times MG_{408}$, $MU_{11} \times MG_{414}$, $MU_{11} \times MG_{408}$, $MU_{11} \times$ NB_4D_2, $MU_{303} \times MG_{414}$, $MU_{303} \times MG_{408}$ and PM $\times$ MG_{408} were found to excel the other hybrids (Table 2.8).

Pupation Rate

Pupation rate was observed to be much higher in all the three multivoltine parental races with a range of values from 90.00% (MU_{303}) to 91.03% (MU_1) compared to the control Pure Mysore (86.51%). Similarly, all the three bivoltine parental races were found to be marginally better with a range of values from 88.39% (MU_{852}) to 89.51% (MG_{414}) than the control NB_4D_2 (88.35%) (Table 2.1). On the other hand the values obtained for the fifteen new hybrids studied were found to vary from 81.90% (PM $\times$ MG_{408}) to 87.70% ($MU_{303} \times MU_{852}$). Of which, four hybrids $MU_1 \times$ NB_4D_2, $MU_{11} \times NB_4D_2$, $MU_{303} \times MU_{852}$ and $MU_{303} \times NB_4D_2$ were found to excel the other hybrids (Table 2.2).

The analysis of variance computed for this trait revealed highly significant values ($P<0.01$) for all the sources of variations (Table 2.3).

The estimates of general combining ability revealed the variability ranging from –1.83 (PM) to 1.02 (MU_{303}) among the multivoltine lines and from –0.10 (MG_{408}) to 1.59 (NB_4D_2) among bivoltine testers. The multivoltine lines MU_1, MU_{11}, MU_{303} and the bivoltine testers MU_{852}, NB_4D_2 were found to be average general combiners. While, the remaining parental races were found to be poor general combiners (Table 2.4).

The specific combining ability effects estimated for sixteen hybrids, recorded in Table 2.5 were found to vary from –0.86 (PM × MG_{408}) to 1.30 (PM × NB_4D_2). Out of sixteen hybrids, eight hybrids were found to express positive values for this trait. Of which only two hybrids MU_1 ×MG_{414} and PM × NB_4D_2 were found to be average specific combiners, while, the remaining hybrids were found to be poor specific combiners.

The analysis of variance computed for the combining ability was found to reveal highly significant variations ($P<0.01$) for crosses, testers, while non-significant variations ($P>0.01$) for Lines and Line × Tester (Table 2.6).

The heterosis for this trait was found to be negative and non significant in all the hybrids values ranging from –6.60 (PM × MG_{108}) to –0.85 (PM × NB_4D_2) (Table 2.7), Similarly the over dominance was also found to be negative and non significant in all the hybrids with values ranging from –7.85 (PM ×MG_{408}) to –1.89 (PM – NB_4D_2) (Table 2.8).

The over all result of the mean performance of the parental races, their hybrids, general combining ability of the parental races, specific combining ability as well as heterosis and over dominance of the hybrids for eleven economic traits were considered in order to identify superior hybrid combinations.

All the three multivoltine parental races viz MU_1, MU_{11}, MU_{303} and the bivoltine parental races MU_{852}, MU_{414}, MG_{408} were found to express higher values for all the eleven economic traits considered in the study than their respective control races Pure Mysore and NB_4D_2. (Table 2.1). Similarly, most of the hybrids were found to express higher mean values for most of the characters than the control hybrid PM × NB_4D_2. Further, seven hybrids MU_1× MU_{852}, MU_1× MG_{414}, MU_1× NB_4D_2, MU_{11}× NB_4D_2, MU_{303} × MU_{852}, MU_{11}× MU_{852} and MU_{303} × MG_{414} were found to express higher values for more than seven of the eleven economic traits considered. It is pertinent to note that the hybrid $MU_{303}\times MU_{852}$ express higher value for all the eleven traits followed by $MU_1 \times MG_{414}$, $MU_1 \times NB_4D_2$ for nine traits, $MU_1 \times MU_{852}$, $MU_{852} \times NB_4D_2$ for eight traits and $MU_1 \times MU_{852}$, MU_{303} MG_{414} for seven traits (Table 2.2).

With reference to the general specific combining ability effect, the multivoltine lines MU_1 and MU_{11} and the bivoltine tester MU_{852} were considered as good general combines and the line MU_{303} and the tester NB_4D_2, as average general combiners for most of the characters considered in the study. While, PM, MG_{414} and MG_{408} were found to be poor general combiners (Table 2.4). Similarly, most of the hybrids were found to express higher values for specific combining ability effects for most of the characters, out of which four hybrids $MU_1 \times MU_{852}$, $MU_1 \times MG_{414}$, $MU_{11} \times MU_{852}$ and $MU_{303} \times MU_{852}$ were found to excel the others and were considered as good specific combiners followed by five hybrids $MU_{11} \times MG_{408}$, $MU_{303} \times NB_4D_2$ PM $\times MG_{408}$ and PM $\times NB_4D_2$ which can be considered as average general combiners. While the remaining seven hybrids were found to be poor specific combiners as they were found to express poor specific combining ability effect (Table 2.5).

With regard to heterosis effect, most of the hybrids were found to express higher values, of which nine hybrids viz $MU_1 \times MU_{852}$, $MU_1 \times NB_4D_2$, $MU_{11} \times MU_{852}$, $MU_{11} \times NB_{4D2}$, $MU_{303}\times MU_{852}$, PM $\times MU_{852}$, PM $\times MG_{414}$, PM $\times MG_{408}$ and PM $\times NB_4D_2$ were found to excel the other hybrids expressing higher values for more than seven of the eleven traits studies followed by six hybrids expressing higher values for more than six traits and only one hybrid for more than five traits (Table 2.7). On the other hand, the over dominance effect studied in sixteen hybrids reveal that six hybrids $MU_1 \times MU_{852}$, $MU_{11} \times MU_{852}$, $MU_1 \times NB_4D_2$, $MU_{303} \times NB_4D_2$, PM $\times MU_{11}$ and PM NB_4D_2 were found to express higher values for more than seven of the eleven traits considered (Table 2.8).

On the basis of the over all results, based on the mean performance of the hybrids, their specific combining ability effect as well the heterosis and over dominance studied for eleven economic traits studied, four hybrids viz MU_1 ´ MU_{852} MU_{11} × MG_{414}, MU_{11} × MU_{852} and MU_{303} × MU_{852} were considered as superior hybrid combinations. The photograph of the cocoons of the above hybrids are depicted in Plate 2.1.

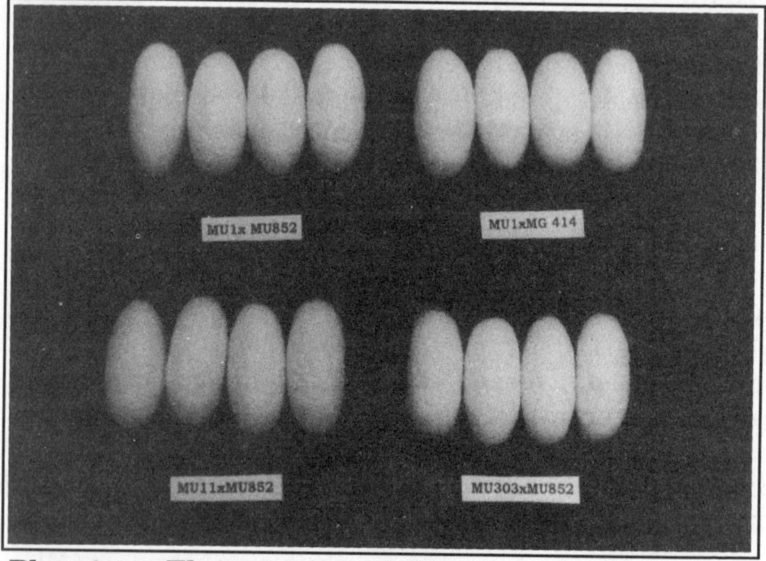

Plate 2.1: The cocoons of four promising multi X bihybrids

DISCUSSION

The domesticated silkworm *Bornbyx mori* in view of its economic importance has attracted the attention of animal breeders in several sericultural countries. The conventional breeding methods undertaken to improve the productivity have resulted in the large number of inbred lines with distinct genotypic and phenotypic differences. Even though, the inbred lines are superior, they will not have much value, if their superiority is not reflected in the hybrids. Therefore, the ultimate results in silkworm breeding are judged by the excellency of the commercial traits of the parental races that appear in the F_1 hybrid. Further, conventional breeding methods are not only directed to the development of new breeds, but also to identify the promising hybrid combinations for commercial exploitation.

The F_1 hybrids were found to be better than their parents in most of the characters of commercial importance (Hirobe, 1967; Kobayashi *et al.*, 1968; Maribashetty *et al.*, 1991; Bhargava *et al*, 1992; Kalpana, 1992; Nirmal Kumar, 1995; Kalappa, 1996; Nanjundaswamy, 1997; and Veeraiah, 1999). The superiority of the hybrids over parental strains is undoubtedly due to the high magnitude of heterosis for most of the characters (Osawa and Harada, 1994; Harada, 1949, 1952, 1954, 1956, 1961; Hirobe and Ohi, 1954; Yokoyama, 1957, 1962; Harada et al., 1961; Takashi, 1968; Gamo, 1976 and Hirobe, 1985). Toyama's (1905) findings on the superiority of the hybrids, a remarkable progress has been made in the spread and growth of sericulture industry (Yokoyama, 1974; Hirobe, 1985; Grekov and Petkov, 1989). This has stimulated many silkworm breeders to undertake extensive research to identify new hybrid combinations for commercial exploitation indifferent regions and seasons.

However, in India due to the limited number of silkworm stocks available only four multi × hi hybrids such as PM × NB_4D_2, PM × NB_7, PM × KA and PM × NB_{18} were developed and identified for commercial exploitation in different parts of the country irrespective of regions and seasons. Moreover the later three hybrids were withdrawn due to certain defects. At present only one multi × bi hybrid namely PM × NB_4D_2 is being exploited in almost all the southern sericultural states of the country including Rayalaseema region of Andhra Pradesh. Even though, some improvement in the productivity of the silk was noticed during the last 2 to 3 decades, the quality of the silk produced rather remain to be poor due to the inherent defects of the Pure Mysore that are passed on to the hybrids. Several attempts made to replace the existing multi × bi hybrid PM × NB_4D_2. have met with little success (Scngupta, 1969; Narasimhanna, 1976; Jolly, 1983; Datta, 1984; Pershad et ah, 1986; Datta and Pershad, 1988 and Bhargava et al., 1992).

During the last few years, the efforts of silkworm breeders in the country have resulted in the development of large number of multivoltine and bivoltine races. However, systematic efforts to develop promising hybrids are wanting.

The present investigation deals with the evaluation of the three new multivolitine races MU_1, MU_{11}, MU_{303} and three new bivoltine races MU_{852}, MG_{414}, MG_{408} along with the respective control Pure Mysore and NB_4D_2 to evaluate their genetic work and use them in appropriate hybrid combinations. Systematic procedures such as the estimation of general combining ability of the parental races as well the specific combining ability, heterosis and over dominance of the hybrids have been undertaken by following Line × Tester analysis proposed by Kempthorne in 1957. The evaluation has helped in understanding the general fitness of the hybrids with consequential improvement in productivity. The pattern of inheritance of the quantitative traits analysed, the complicating effects of gene interaction and the influence of the environmental factors on the expression of the traits even though rather difficult to understand the number and nature of genes that contribute to the phenotypic effect. The utilization of the known and established silkworm races in the study has made it possible to realize the objective of synthesizing the promising multi × bi commercial hybrids, which can be exploited in Rayalaseema region of Andhra Pradesh.

The results obtained are discussed separately with respect to each one of the characters analysed.

Fecundity

The number of eggs laid by the female moth is referred to as fecundity. The fecundity varies in multivoltine, bivoltine and univoltine races. In addition, it is also variable with in themselves depending on the nutritional as well the environmental factors during mating and oviposition (Hussanein and Sharawwy, 1960, 1962; Yokoyama, 1963, 1973; Narayanan *et al.,* 1964; Jolly *et al.*, 1966; Sidhu *et al.*, 1969; Ueda *et al.*, 1969, 1971, 1975; Kovalov, 1970; Sengupta *et al.*, 1974; Pillai and Krishnaswami, 1987). Further, the egg laying capacity of a particular race/breed is dependent on the genotype of the mother moth also. It is also established that hybrids were found to be superior than the pure races in the egg laying capacity.

The superior fecundity observed in the multivoltine and bivoltine parental races over their respective controls in the present study clearly reflects their genetic constitution (Table 2.1). Similarly, the increased fecundity of the fourteen of the fifteen new hybrids studied over the control (Table 2.2) indicate their genetic advantage and is in conformity with the findings of Benchamin and Krishnaswami (198la and b).

The high estimates obtained for general combining ability for multivoltine control Pure Mysore compared to other multivoltine lines and bivoltine testers can be attributed to its genetic constitution (Table 2.4). Similarly, the positive specific combining ability effects obtained in eleven of the sixteen hybrids indicate their ability to combine well in the hybrids and is in conformity with the observations of Jolly *et al.,* 1966 (Table 2.5), who demonstrated the additive gene action in the hybrids for this trait. The marginal differences observed between the hybrids reflect the genetic diversity of the parents in question.

The insignificant values observed for heterosis and over dominance for this trait in most of the hybrids reflect the absence of heterotic effect. The higher fecundity observed in some of the parental races as well some of the hybrids simply reflect the genetic background of the females rather than the effect of heterosis and over dominance and contradict the findings of Watanabe (1961), Tayade (1987), Chandrashekaraiah (1992) and Malik (1992), who reported the heterosis and over-dominance for this trait among the hybrid combinations in bivoltine races (Table 2.7 and 2.8).

Hatching Percentage

Hatching percentage is an important parameter cannoting the viability of the eggs. The duration of mating is known to affect this trait irrespective of their voltinism (Narayanan *et al.,* 1964 and Petkov *et al.,* 1979). This trait is largely dependent on the physiological status of both male and females as well the environmental factors (Tazima 1962).

The superiority observed in the multivoltine and bivoltine parental races over their respective control races clearly reflects their genetic constitution (Table 2.1). Similarly, the increased hatching percentage observed in seven of the fifteen new hybrids studied, than the control hybrid indicate its genetic superiority (Table 2.2).

The high estimates obtained for general combining ability for the bivoltine tester MG_{414} compared to other bivoltine testers and multivoltine lines can be ascribed to its favourable genetic constitution (Table 2.4) Similarly, moderate to high specific combining ability effects obtained in most of the hybrids indicate their ability to combine with the hybrids. The variability in the magnitude of specific combining ability exhibiting both the positive and negative effects among the hybrids studied (Table 2.5) reflect on the genetic diversity.

The insignificant values observed for heterosis and over dominance for this trait in most of the hybrids reflect the absence of heterotic effect. The higher hatching percentage observed in some of the parental races as well in some of the hybrids reflect the genetic background and physiological status of the female rather than the expression of heterosis and over dominance and is in conformity with the findings of Nacheva (1980), who demonstrated increased hybrid vigour in the hybrids for this trait.

Larval Duration

Larval duration is an important attribute of economic value. The hybrids generally have a shorter larval duration than the pure races. In general, the larval duration is influenced both by genetic factors and environmental factors such as nutrition, temperature and photoperiod. In addition, over crowding of the larval population affect the competing ability of the larvae with concomitant decrease in the rate of development increasing the larval duration.

The superiority observed in both multivoltine and bivoltine parental races for this trait over their respective control races clearly reflects their genetic constitution (Table 2.1). Similarly, the shorter larval duration observed in all the fifteen new hybrids studied than the control hybrid indicate its genetic superiority (Table 2.2) and parallels the findings of Singh and Hirobe, 1964 ; Krishnaswaini and Narasimhanna, 1974; Tayade,1987; Udupa and Gowda,1988; Subba Rao and Sahai, 1989; Satenahalli *et al.,* 1989; Rayar and Govindan, 1990; Raju, 1990; Kalpana, 1992; Chandrashekaraiah, 1992, Nirmal Kumar, 1995 and Nanjundaswamy, 1997.

Since the shorter larval duration is advantageous, the negative values were considered in calculating the general combining ability, specific combining ability, heterosis and over dominance.

The high estimates obtained for general combining ability for the multivoltine lines MU_1, MU_{11} and bivoltine testers MU_{852}, NB_4D_2 compared to other multivoltine lines and bivoltine testers can be ascribed to their genetic endowment for this trait (Table 2.4). Similarly the high specific combining ability effect obtained in eleven of sixteen hybrids studied (Table 2.5) indicate their ability to combine with the hybrids, thus establishing the presence of favorable gene combinations and is in conformity with the observations of Garno and Hirabayashi(1983); Subba Rao and Sahai (1989), who demonstrated the additive gene action for this trait in the hybrids.

The significant values observed for heterosis in all the hybrids and over dominance in fourteen of the sixteen hybrids studied for this trait indicate their superiority (Table 2.7 and 2.8) and is in conformity with the findings of Yokoyama, 1957; Tayade, 1987; Datta and Pershad, 1988; Subba Rao and Sahai, 1989; Malik, 1992 and Nanjundaswamy, 1997.

Larval Weight

Larval weight is one of the important parameter which determines not only the health of the larvae, but also the quality of the cocoons spun (Matsumura and Takeuchi, 1950).

The superiority observed in the multivoltine and bivoltine parental races over their respective controls clearly reflect their genetic constitution for this trait. (Table 2.1). Similarly, the increased larval weight in the twelve of fifteen new hybrids studied than the control hybrid (Table 2.2) indicate their genetic superiority and is in support of the observations of Nacheva (1980). Further the correlation between the larval weight and cocoon weight has been clearly established in the present study and is in conformity with the findings of Watanabe, 1961; Ueda ct al.,1969, 1971, 1975; Kasturi Dai, 1983 and Pai, 1988 and contradicts the observations of Chandrashekaraiah, 1992, who reported the non-correlation between larval weight and cocoon weight in his study.

The high estimates obtained for general combining ability for multivoltine lines MU_1 and MU_{303} and the bivoltine testers MU_{852} and MG_{408} compared to other multivoltine lines and bivoltine testers can be ascribed to their genetic constitution (Table 2.4). Similarly high estimates of specific combining ability effect obtained in nine of the sixteen hybrids studied (Table 2.5) indicate their ability to combine well with the hybrids and is in conformity with the findings of Chandrashekaraiah, 1992, who demonstrated the additive gene action for this trait in the hybrids.

The significant values observed in fifteen of the sixteen hybrids for heterosis and in all the hybrids for over dominance for this trait indicating their superiority (Tables 2.7 and 2.8) and thus parallels the observations of Sreerama Reddy et al (1986), Rayar and Govindan (1990).

Cocoon Yield by Number

It is an important parameter contributing to viability. The superiority observed for this trait in the multivoltine and bivoltine parental races over their respective controls clearly reflects their genetic constitution (Table 2.1). While the increase in cocoon yield by number even though is noticed in all the new hybrids, the significant increase observed in only four of the fifteen hybrids indicate the favourable and most favourable gene combination for this trait in the respective hybrids (Table 2.2).

The high estimates obtained for the general combining ability for the multivoltine lines MU_{11}, MU_{303} and Pure Mysore and bivoltine tester NB_4D_2 compared to other multivoltine lines and bivoltine testers can be ascribed to their genetic endowment for this trait (Table 2.4). Similarly seven of the sixteen hybrids studied for specific combining ability effect indicate their ability to combine well with the hybrids thus establishing the presence of favourable genetic constitution for this trait (Table 2.5).

The significant value obtained for eight of the sixteen hybrids studied for heterosis and in all the hybrids for over-dominance effect for this trait indicate their superiority (Tables 2.7 and 2.8) and is in conformity with the findings of Sidhu *et al.*, 1969; Sengupta *et al.*, 1974; Iyengar *et al.*,1083; Raju, 1990; Knlpana,1992 and Kalappa, 1996, who reported positive heterosis and over dominance for this trail in the hybrids.

Cocoon Yield by Weight

It is an important trait contributing to productivity. The superiority observed in the multivoltine and bivoltine parental races over their respective controls clearly reflects their genetic endowment for this trait (Table 2.1). Similarly, the increased cocoon yield by weight in ten of the fifteen new hybrids studied, over the control hybrid (Table 2.2) indicate their genetic superiority and parallels the findings of Sidhu et al., 1969; Krishnaswami and Tikoo, 1971 and Kumar, 1995.

The higher estimates obtained for general combining ability for multivoltine lines MU_1 and MU_{11} than the other multivoltine lines and bivoltine testers can be ascribed to their genetic constitution (Table 2.4). Similarly, high estimates of specific combining ability effect obtained in eleven of the Sixteen hybrids studied (Table 2.5) indicate their ability to combine well with the hybrids.

The significant values observed in all the hybrids for heterosis and over dominance for this trait indicate their superiority (Tables 2.7 and 2.8) and is in conformity with the findings of Yokoyama, 1957; Sengupta *et al.*, 1974;Vijaya Raghavan and Das, 1992 and Nanjundaswamy, 1997, Who reported positive heterosis and over dominance among the hybrids for this trait.

Cocoon Weight

Cocoon weight is an important attribute of silkworm and is found to vary in different races.

The superiority in the cocoon weight observed in the multivoltine and bivoltine parental races over their respective controls clearly reflects their genetic constitution (Table 2.1). Similarly the increased cocoon weight observed in thirteen of the fifteen new hybrids studied over the control hybrid (Table 2.2) indicate their genetic superiority and support the observations of Krishnaswami *et al.,* 1964; Sengupta *et al.*, 1974; Tayade, 1986; Raje Urs, 1988; Govindan *et al.*,1990; Raju, 1990 and Satenahalli *et al.,* 1990. Further the correlation between the larval weight and cocoon weight has been clearly established in the present study and is in conformity the findings of Watanabe, 1961; Ueda *et al*., 1969, 1971, 1975; Kasturi Bai, 1983 and Pal, 1988 and is contrary to the findings of Chandrashekaraiah, 1992, who reported the non-correlation between larval weight and cocoon weight in his study.

The high estimates obtained for general combining ability in the multivoltine line MU_1 and bivoltine tester NB_4D_2 compared to other multivoltine lines and bivoltine testers can be ascribed to their genetic background (Table 2.4). Similarly, high estimates of specific combining ability effect obtained in thirteen of the sixteen hybrids studied indicate their ability to combine well with the hybrids (Table 2.5) and is in conformity with the findings of Narasimhanna and Rajashekarashetty (1979), who demonstrated predominant non additive gene action as well epistasis for this trait.

The significant values obtained in all the sixteen hybrids for heterosis and over dominance effect for this trait indicate their superiority (Tables 2.7 and 2.8) and is in support of the view that the phenomenon of heterosis could be either due to additive gene action or due to the dominant hypothesis as reported by Nacheva, 1980; Petkov and Nacheva, 1987 and Petkov, 1989.

Shell Weight

The shell weight is an important economic character of commercial value. It is known to vary in different races and also under different rearing conditions as well as nutritional status of the mulberry leaf during growth and development of larvae.

The superiority in shell weight observed in both the multivoltine and bivoltine parental races over their respective controls clearly reflects their genetic constitution (Table 2.1). Similarly, the increased shell weight observed in thirteen of the fifteen new hybrids studied over the control hybrid (Table 2.2) indicate their genetic advantage.

The high estimate of general combining ability values obtained for multivoltine line MU_1 and bivoltine tester MU_{852} compared to other multivoltine lines and bivoltine testers can be ascribed to its genetic endowment (Table 2.4). Similarly, high estimates of specific combining ability effect obtained in ten of the fifteen new hybrids studied indicate their ability to combine well with the hybrids (Table 2.5) and thus parallels the observations of Narasimhanna and Rajashekarashetty, 1979; Gamo and Hirabayashi, 1983; Chandrashekaraiah, 1992 and Subba Rao and Sahai, 1989, who reported the additive gene action in the hybrids for this trait.

The significant values obtained in all the sixteen hybrids for heterotic effect for this trait (Table 2.7) can be attributed to the allelic interaction and is in conformity with the findings of Krishnaswami *et al.*, 1964; Raje Urs, 1988 and Satenehalli *et al.*,1990 in mulberry silkworm and also with the observations of Jolly *et al.*, 1969 in non-mulberry tasar silkworm and contradict the observations of Narasirnhanna, 1976 and Raju, 1990, who demonstrated that the low degree of heterosis in the hybrids for this trait. On the other hand, only two of the sixteen hybrids studied for over dominance effect reveal significant values (Table 2.8) indicating the absence of over dominance effect for this traits in the majority of hybrids and is in conformity with the findings of Narasirnhanna, 1970 and Raju, 1990, who demonstrated low degree of over dominance in the hybrid.

Shell Ratio

Shell ratio is an important parameter contributing to productivity. It is known to vary in different races/breeds. The superiority for shell ratio observed in the multivoltine and bivoltine parental races over their respective controls clearly reflects their genetic constitution (Table 2.1). Similarly, the increased shell ratio of the seven of fifteen new hybrids over the control hybrid (Table 2.2) indicate their genetic superiority and is in conformity with the findings of Krishnaswami *et al*., (1964).

The high estimates obtained for general combining ability for bivoltine tester MU_{852} compared to other bivoltine testers and multivoltine lines can be ascribed to its genetic constitution (Table 2.4). Similarly, high estimates of specific combining ability effect obtained in ten of the sixteen hybrids studied indicate their ability to combine well in the hybrids (Table 2.5) and is in conformity with the observations of Narsimhanna and Rajashekarashetty, 1979; Gamo and Hirabayashi, 1983 and Subba Rao, 1983, who reported the additive gene action for this trait.

The significant values obtained in thirteen of sixteen hybrids studied for heterosis (Table 2.7) and for all the hybrids for over dominance effect for this trait (Table 2.8) indicate their superiority and the results are in conformity with the observations of Nanjundaswamy (1997) and contrary to the findings of Subba Rao and Sahai (1989) who reported negative heterosis and over dominance in the hybrids for this trait.

Silk Filament Length

Length of the silk filament is considered to be important quantitative trait in silkworm (Miyahara, 1978;

Yokoyama, 1979). Longer the silk filament, greater is the benefit to the reeling industry. Hence the improvement of silk filament is an important objective in silk worm breeding programme. The superiority for silk filament length observed in the multivoltine and bivoltine parental races over their respective control races clearly indicate their genetic endowment (Table 2.1). While, only five of the fifteen new hybrids studied, were observed to have longer silk filament length than the control hybrid (Table 2.2) clearly indicating the favourable combination involved in the expression of this trait and is in support of the observations of Krishnaswami and Narasimhanna, 1974; Raju, 1990 and Chandrashekaraiah, 1992.

The high estimates of general combining ability effect obtained for multtivoltine lines $MU_{303,}$ Pure Mysore and bivoltine testers MU_{852}, NB_4D_2 compared to other multivoltine lines and bivoltine testers can be ascribed to their genetic constitution (Table 2.4). Similarly high estimates of specific combining ability effect obtained in ten of sixteen hybrids studied indicate their ability to combine well in the hybrids (Table 2.5) and is in conformity with the observation of Gamo and Hirabayashi, 1983; Kantarathnakul et al., 1987; Subba Rao and Sahai, 1989, who reported the additive gene action for this trait.

The significant values obtained in all the sixteen hybrids for heterosis and over dominance (Table 2.7 and 2.8) for this trait indicate their superiority and parallels the findings of Nacheva (1980) and Nanjundaswamy (1997) and contrary to the observations of Subba Rao and Sahai (1989), who demonstrated negative heterosis for this trait.

Pupation Rate

It is an important parameter cannoting the viability. The superiority for pupation rate observed in the multi-voltine and bivoltine parental races over their respective control races clearly indicate their genetic endowment (Table 2.1).

Similarly, the increased pupation rate observed in four of the fifteen new hybrids studied over the control hybrid for this trait indicate the involvement of favourable gene combination and thus parallel the findings of Sidhu et al., 1968 and Kovalov, 1970 (Table 2.2).

The insignificant general combining ability effect observed for all the multivoltine lines and bivoltine testers indicate the absence of general combining ability effect for this trait (Table 2.4). While, the high estimates of specific combining ability effect observed in eight of the sixteen hybrids studied (Table 2.5) indicate their superiority for this trait.

The non-significant values obtained for heterosis and over dominance for this trait in all the hybrids studied indicate the absence of heterotic and over dominance effect (Tables 2.7 and 2.8) and thus contradict the observation of Kalpana, 1992; Nirmal Kumar, 1995 and Nanjundaswamy, 1997 who reported positive values among the hybrids for this trait.

On the basis of the foregoing discussion of the performance of new hybrids and controls, general combining ability of the parental races and specific combining ability as well the heterosis and over-dominance of the hybrids observed with respect to each one of the traits, it is possible to determine the promising multi bi hybrid combinations. Further, the lesser degree of variability in the manifestation of most of the characters in the hybrids than the parental races is one of the desirable features for commercial exploitation of the hybrids as evidenced by the mean values obtained for various traits. Superiority observed in all the three multivoltine parental races MU_1, MU_{11}, MU_{303} and the bivoltine parental races MU_{852}, MG_{414}, MG_{408} over their respective control races Pure Mysore and NB_4D_2 for all the traits indicate the superiority of these races (Table 2.1). Similarly, the increased values observed for more than seven of the eleven economic traits in seven of the fifteen new hybrids viz $MU_1 \times M_{852}$, $MU_1 \times MG_{414}$, MU_1,× NB_4D_2, $MU_{11}\times NB_4D_2$, $MU_{303} \times MU_{852}$, $MU_{11} \times$ and $MU_{852} \times MU_{303} \times MG_{414}$ indicate the superiority of these hybrids over the others (Table 2.2).

The high estimates of general combining ability effect obtained for MU_1, MU_{11} among multivoltine lines and bivoltine tester MU_{852} compared to other multivoltine lines and bivoltine testers reflect their good general combining ability and can be ascribed to their genetic constitution. While, the remaining parental races were found to be average/poor general combiners indicating their inability to combine well with others (Table 2.4). Similarly, high estimates of specific combining ability effect obtained in four of the sixteen hybrids studied viz $MU_1 \times MU_{852}$, $MU_1 \times MG_{414}$, $MU_{11} \times MU_{852}$ and $MU_{303} \times MU_{852}$ indicate their ability to combine well with the hybrids (Table 2.5). It is interesting to note that al the above hybrids were found to excel other hybrids not only for specific combining ability effect but also for mean performance. While the remaining hybrids were either average/poor specific combiners with average/poor specific combining ability effect for most of the traits considered in the study.

On the other hand, the studies on the heterosis in sixteen hybrids reveal high estimates of heterotic effect in nine of the sixteen hybrids exhibiting hybrid vigour. Similarly, six of the sixteen hybrids exhibiting higher value for more than seven of the eleven economic traits indicate their superiority. It is interesting to point out that the four hybrids $MU_1 \times MU_{852}$, $MU_1 \times MG_{414}$, $MU_{11} \times MU_{852}$, and $MU_{303} \times MU_{852}$ were identified as the most superior hybrid combinations in view of their high mean performance, specific combining ability as well the magnitude of heterosis and over dominance. Hence they were adjudicated as the most promising multi-bi-hybrids suitable for commercial exploitation.

SUMMARY

1. Three new multivoltine races MU_1, MU_{11}, MU_{303} and three new bivoltine races MU_{852}, MG_{414}, MG_{408} were used as parental races in the hybridization programme. The suitability of the above races to the Rayalaseema region form the basis (Chapter 1) for their utilization in making crosses and to understand their genetic worth with regard to the general and specific combining ability as well the magnitude of the heterosis and over dominance expressed in the hybrids.
2. A reliable method, Line × Tester analysis was employed by utilizing the multivoitines as lines and bivoltines as testers. A total of sixteen hybrid combinations were derived including the control hybrid PM × NB_4D_2. All the hybrids and their parents were reared in replicates of three each by following the standard rearing techniques, feeding the mulberry leaf harvested from M_5 garden maintained in the university campus by following the recommended package of practices.
3. The performance of the parental races as well the hybrids were analyzed by evaluating the expression of eleven economic characters such as fecundity, hatching percentage, larval duration, larval weight, cocoon yield by number, cocoon yield by weight, cocoon weight, shell weight, shell ratio, silk filament length and pupation rate. The mean of the replicates for each one of the characters was pooled separately for the parental as well hybrids and subjected to relevant statistical analysis to evaluate the general performance of the parental races and their hybrids. The general combining ability of the parental races, the specific combining ability as well the heterosis and over-dominance of the hybrids were evaluated in order to understand the ability of the new races to combine well with the others and express the profitable amounts of hybrid vigour.

4. Analysis of variance computed to estimate the combining ability reveals large mean sum of squares for the traits analyzed for lines, testers and Line × Testers indicting their genetic diversity. The higher degree of manifestation observed in the combining ability of the new lines and testers can be attributed to their genetic endowment which was found to combine favourably in the hybrids resulting the gene interaction and phenotypic expression with regard to most of the traits analyzed.
5. Of the fifteen new hybrids, seven hybrids such as $MU_1 \times MU_{852}$, $MU_1 \times MG_{414}$, $MU_1 \times NB_4D_2$, $MU_{11} \times NB_4D_2$, $MU_{303} \times MU_{852}$, $\times$ MG_{414} were found to excel the other hybrids as well the control hybrid $PM \times NB_4D_2$ for more than seven of the eleven economic traits studied, thus establish their superiority over others. The higher values observed for most of the characters in the new multivoltine and bivoltine races as well in the new hybrids confer their superiority over their respective parental races as well the control hybrid.
6. The positive values of general combining ability estimates for most of the characters in all the parental races indicate their inherent potential to combine well and yield desirable levels of superiority in the expression of the economic characters analyzed.
7. The manifestation of specific combining ability observed in the hybrids revealed a high magnitude of the specific combining ability effect for more than seven of the eleven economic traits analyzed in four hybrids such as $MU_1 \times MU_{852}$, $MU_1 \times MG_{414}$, $MU_{11} \times MU_{852}$ and $MU_{303} \times MU_{852}$.
8. The high degree of heterosis was observed in nine hybrids such as MU_1, MU_{852}, $MU_1 \times NB_4D_2$, $MU_{11} \times MU_{852}$, $MU_{11} \times NB_4D_2$, $MU_{303} \times MU_{852}$, $PM \times MU_{852}$, $PM \times MG_{414}$, $PM \times MG_{408}$ and $PM \times NB_4D_2$. Similarly, high

degree of over dominance was observed in six hybrids such as $MU_1 \times MU_{852}$, $MU_{11} \times MU_{852}$, $MU_{11} \times NB_4D_2$, $MU_{303} \times NB_4D_2$, PM MU_{852}, and PM $\times$ NB_4D_2 for more than seven of the eleven economic traits, The four hybrids viz, $MU_1 \times MU_{852}$, $MU_1 \times MG_{414}$, $MU_{11} \times MU_{852}$ and $MU_{303} \times MU_{852}$ which were shown to posses a high degree of specific combining ability were also found to excel in the expression of heterosis and over-dominance.

9. On the basis of the mean performance of the new hybrids, general combining ability of the parental races, specific combining ability as well the heterosis and over dominance of the hybrids, four hybrids viz $MU_1 \times MU_{852}$, $MU_1 \times MG_{414}$, $MU_{11} \times MU_{852}$ and $MU_{303} \times MU_{852}$ are identified as, superior to other hybrids and the control. In view of this they are adjudicated as the most promising multi $\times$ bi hybrids suitable for commercial exploitation in the Rayalaseema region of Andhra Pradesh.

Chapter 3

FIELD STUDIES ON THE PERFORMANCE OF THE PROMISING HYBRIDS AND THEIR ADJUDICATION

INTRODUCTION

Silk worm breeds developed under laboratory conditions however superior they may be need to be tested in the field conditions in order to qualify them for commercial rearing. Almost all the characters of commercial importance in silkworm are under the influence of complex interaction between the blocks of polygenes and the dynamic environmental conditions to which they are exposed during growth and development. Therefore, the performance of the breed is not only dependent on the genetic architecture but also on the quality of the rearing environment as well the nutritional status of mulberry leaf. In view of the above, efforts are being made to integrate the genetic potential of the silkworm breeds and their response to the environmental conditions. The proper understanding of this has lead to the development of skills in the management of mulberry garden and silkworm rearing. The laboratory conditions in which the new multi × bi hybrids are developed are different from those prevailing in the field. Therefore, it is of utmost importance to undertake a study on the performance of the new hybrids under the environmental conditions prevailing at the farmers level in order to understand the phenotypic expression of the commercial characters. Such a study not only helps in understanding the performance of the breeds but also helps in assessing their feasibility for commercial exploitation.

In view of the above, the present investigation was undertaken to understand the performance of the four new multi × bivoltine hybrids synthesized and identified (Chapter 2) in order to adjudicate most promising multi x bi hybrids for commercial exploitation in the Rayalaseema region of Andhra Pradesh.

Hybrids viz. $MU_1 \times MU_{852}$, $MU_1 \times MG_{414}$, $\times MU_{11} \times MU_{852}$ and $MU_{303} \times MU_{852}$ developed and identified as superior hybrid combinations (Chapter 2) along with the control hybrid PM × NB_4D_2 form the material for the field study. The laboratory performance of the above hybrids is described in Chapter 2.

The seed cocoons of the parental races harvested were kept separately for moth emergence. Male and female moths are separated. The females of multivoltine and males of bivoltine were allowed to mate for three hours. After effective mating the males and females were separated. Females were allowed for egg laying under dark condition for 24 hours. After oviposition the females were subjected to moth examination to ensure disease freeness. 30-35 dfls of each one of the hybrid were prepared. 20 dfls of each one of the hybrid were supplied to each one of the four selected farmers in a village near the university campus to be reared simultaneously along with the control hybrid PM $\times NB_4 D_2$, the layings of which were supplied by the Government grainage, The village is located about 20 kms from Tirupathi. The four farmers were identified and selected with the help of the staff of department of sericulture, Andhra Pradesh. All the farmers are sufficiently experienced and maintain roughly about 1-2 acres of mulberry garden following standard package of practices with assured irrigation facility.

The rearing was conducted simultaneously by all the farmers following the standard rearing practices generally adopted by the farmers. The cocoons were harvested on 5th day of spinning and were taken to cocoon market for disposal.

The study was conducted in two trials in order to make sure of the performance of the new multi × bi hybrids along with the control. The data generated from both the trails with particular reference to cocoon yield was collected and converted for 100 dfls. The results obtained were assembled and shown in Tables 3.1 to 3.4 along with the rate fetched per kg of cocoons and subjected to statistical analysis.

Statistical Methods

The performance of the new hybrids studied in two field traits was analysed to calculate the percentage of increment/decrement over the control hybrid by employing the formula as follows.

$$\frac{X-Y}{Y} \times 100$$

Where

X = the object compared

Y = the compared ones.

RESULTS

The cocoon yield and the rate of cocoons per kg for each one of the hybrids reared separately by four different farmers along with the control, the percentage of increment/decrement is presented in Tables 3.1 to 3.4.

Table 3.1: Comparison of the Field Performance of the New Hybrid MU_1 □ MU_{852} Over the Control

Trial No.	Hybrid Name	No. of dfls	Actual yield supplied	Yield/ 100 dfls (kg)	Increment/ Decrement (kg)	Rate/kg (Rs.) (%)
1.	$MU_1 \times MU_{852}$	20	11.3	56.5	34.52	76.75
	$PM \times NB_4D_2$	150	63	42	-V	62.50
2.	$MU_1 \times MU_{852}$	20	11.5	57.5	35.29	78.20
	$PM \times NB_4D_2$	175	74.47	42.5	–	62.00

Table 3.2: Comparison of the Field Performance of the New Hybrid MU_1 □ MU_{414} Over the Control

Trial No.	Hybrid Name	No. of dfls supplied	Actual yield (kg)	Yield/ 100 dfls (kg)	Increment/ Decrement (%)	Rate/kg (Rs.)
1.	$MU_1 \times MG_{414}$	20	10.8	54.0	31.06	79.00
	$PM \times NB_4D_2$	175	72.1	41.2	–	64.25
2.	$MU_1 \times MG_{414}$	20	10.9	54.5	30.69	75.60
	$PM \times NB_4D_2$	200	83.4	41.7	–	66.20

Table 3.3: Comparison of the Field Performance of the New Hybrid MU_{11} □ MU_{852} Over the Control

Trial No.	Hybrid Name	No. of dfls supplied	Actual yield (kg)	Yield/ 100 dfls (kg)	Increment/ Decrement (%)	Rate/kg (Rs.)
1.	$MU_{11} \times MU_{852}$	20	11.6	58.0	33.94	75.50
	$PM \times NB_4D_2$	200	86.6	43.3	–	63.50
2.	$MU_{11} \times MU_{852}$	20	11.2	56.0	27.85	77.30
	$PM \times NB_4D_2$	150	65.7	43.8	–	64.40

Table 3.4: Comparison of the Field Performance of the New Hybrid MU_{303} □ MU_{852} Over the Control

Trial No.	Hybrid Name	No. of dfls supplied	Actual yield (kg)	Yield/ 100 dfls (kg)	Increment/ Decrement (%)	Rate/kg (Rs.)
1.	$MU_{303} \times MU_{852}$	20	11.40	57.0	32.55	78.25
	$PM \times NB_4D_2$	175	75.25	43.0	–	63.75
2.	$MU_{303} \times MU_{852}$	20	11.70	58.5	32.65	76.25
	$PM \times NB_4D_2$	150	66.15	44.1	–	62.20

Perusal of the Tables 3.1 to 3.4 clearly reveal a substantial improvement in the yield of the new hybrids varying from 54 kg ($MU_1 \times MG_{414}$) to 58.5 kg ($MU_{303} \times MU_{852}$) compared to the control which vary from 41.2 kg to 44.1 kg ($PM \times NB_4D_2$). Similarly the cocoon of all the hybrids fetched comparatively much higher prices varying from Rs. 75.50/kg ($MU_{11} \times MU_{852}$) to Rs. 79/kg ($MU_1 \times MG_{414}$) compared to control $PM \times NB_4D_2$ which fetched a varying price from Rs. 62.00 to Rs. 66.20/kg.

The over all picture presented in the tables revealed a substantial improvement in the new hybrids varying from 27.85% in $MU_{11} \times MU_{852}$ to 35.29% in1 $\times$ MU_{852} over the control hybrid $PM \times NB_4D_2$.

DISCUSSION

Systematic and planned hybridization together with improved farming and rearing practices have helped a great deal to increase the productivity of silk per unit. The contributions of research and development are universly known in improving the productivity coupled with quality. The quality and the quantity of the product of any industry always play la vital role in its viability. The strategies that encompass the upgradation of the quality and the quantity are many such as varietal improvement, manipulation of rearing environment, prevention of diseases and extension methodologies to name a few. The integration of the concepts and their successful implementation hold the key for success.

Over all improvement in the productivity is dependant on the concomitant improvement in a number of inter related quantitative traits, genotype and environment interactions which rather modify/alter the targeted yield performance. Therefore, the emphasis lies on the genetic stability of the improved varieties since the replacement is not easy to come by in Sericulture as the gestation period for a variety to become popular with farmers enabling them to switch over to the new strains is usually long.

For commercialization, a hybrid has to yield higher quantities of silk than the control. Therefore the performance of a new silkworm hybrid should be relatively high for number of commercial characters. The quantitative traits expressed in an environment and therefore their phenotypic values are a function of genotype and environmental interaction. Therefore, it is necessary to study the performance of the new multi X bi hybrids developed in an environment in which they are commercially exploited. Such a study certainly throw light in understanding the suitability or otherwise of the new breeds to the environment prevailing in a particular area/region.

Tirupathi and its surrounding villages being a part of Rayalaseema region is one of the potential Sericultural areas of Andhra Pradesh. It is rather pertinent to note that even though Sericulture is being practiced in this area for several decades no substantial improvement could be seen. This is perhaps due to the rearing of same multi × bi hybrid, PM × NB_4D_2 which is also being reared in Karnataka and other parts of the country as well.

Sincere attempts to replace this race have not been made to introduce new hybrids which are more productive than PM × NB_4D_2. Therefore the studies on the performance of the four new multi X bi hybrids along with the control such as MU_1 × MU_{852}, MU_1 × MG_{414}, MU_{11} × MU_{852} and MU_{303} × MU_{852} were under taken to assess their feasibility or otherwise to be introduced in this area. Comparison in the yield potential of the new hybrids over the control clearly reflect the superior genetic endowment in the new multi X bi hybrids responding favourably to the conditions prevailing in Rayalaseema region. The study also clearly point out the superiority of the new hybrids in their stability in the expression of economic characters and support the findings of Kogure, 1933; Suzuki, 1954; Narayanan *et al.*, 1967; Krishnaswami et al., 1970a, 1970b; Ueda *et al.*, 1969 and Kobayashi et al., 1986.

The versatility of the new hybrid is also reflected in the significant improvement of the cocoon yield as well the rate fetched per kg. of cocoons thus exhibiting improvement in both the quantity and the quality. These two parameters have substantially contributed to the significant improvement of 27.85% to 34.25% over the control. The improvement in the productivity, quality and profitability observed in the study certainly qualify the new multi x bi hybrids for commercial exploitation in Rayalaseema region making Sericulture a more profitable venture enabling the industry for its all round growth and development.

SUMMARY

1. The field triats of the new multi × bi hybrids were conducted. 20 dfls of each one of the hybrids were supplied to each one of the four different farmers in a village to be reared along with the control hybrid PM × NB_4D_2, the dfls of which were supplied by the Department of Sericulture, Andhra Pradesh.
2. The selected farmers are traditional and experienced and maintain 1-2 acres of mulberry garden following standard package of practices with assured irrigation facilities.
3. The study was conducted twice and the data on the yield of cocoon and the rate fetched as well the percentage of increment/decrement is tabulated.
4. The yield of cocoons per 100 dfls in the new hybrids was observed to be much higher than the control hybrid reflecting their superiority. Similarly the significant increase in the price of cocoons certainly indicate the quality.
5. The significant percentage of increment in the cocoon yield reflect not only the superiority but also contribute to the economic benefits of the farmers.
6. The new hybrids are considered to have the genetic potential which contribute to the productivity, quality and sustainability for growth and development of sericulture in Rayalaseema region of Andhra Pradesh.

BIBLIOGRAPHY

Abadjieva and Radka, 1980. Developing and Maintaining of New Silkworm *Bombyx mori L.* Lines for Industrial Hybridization. Genet. & pi breed. 13(3): 216-222.

Anonymous., 1971. *Sericulture Overseas,* Tectmucal Co-operation Agency, Japan, p. 106.

Barton, N.H., 1986. The Maintenance of Polygenic Variation Through a Balance Between Mutation and Stabilizing Selection. *Genet Res. Camb.* 47: 209-216.

Benchamin, K.V. and S. Krishnaswami., 1981a. Studies on the Egg Production Efficiency in Silkworm *Bombyx mori L.* I. On the Various Factors Contributing to Egg Production. *Proc. Seri. Symp. and Seminar*, TNAU, Coimbatore pp. 1-6.

Benchamin, K.V. and S. Krishnaswami, 1981 b. Studies on the Egg Production Efficiency in Silkworm, *Bombyx mori L.* II. Egg Production Efficiency in Hybrid Parents and Its Effective Application. *Proc. Seri. Symp.* and *Seminar*, TNAU. Coimbatoret pp. 7-14.

Benchamin, K. V. Jolly, M. S. and D.A. I. Benjamin, 1988. Studies on the Reciprocal Crosses of Multivoltine and Bivoltine Breeds in Silkworm *Bombyx mori L.* With Special Reference to the Use of Bivoltine Hybrid as a Parent. *Ind. J. Seric.* 27(1) : 27-34.

Bhargawa, Thiagarajan, V., M. Ramesh Babu and.B. Nagaraj, 1992. Combining Ability and Genetic Analysis of Quantitative Traits in Silkworm *Bombyx mori L. J. Genet & Breed.* 46: 327-330.

Chandrashekaraiah, 1992. Studies on the Genetics of Quantitative Traits in a Few Multivoltine and Bivoltine Races of Silkworm *Bombyx mori L.* Ph.D., Thesis., University of Mysore, Mysore.

Datta, R.K, 1984. Improvement of Silkworm Races (*Bombyx mori L.*) in India. Sericologia, 24(3): 393-415.

Datta, R.K. and G.D. Pershad., 1988. Combining Ability Among Multivoltinc × Blvoltine Silkworm (*Bornbyx mori L.*) Hybrids. *Sericologia*. 28(1): 21-29.

Eberhart, S.A. and Russel, W.A., 1966. Stability Parameters for Comparing Varieties Crop. *Sci.* 6: 36-40.

Freeman, Q.H. and Perkins, J.M., 1971. Environmental and Genotype-environmental Components of Variability. VIII. Relations Between Genotypes Grown in Different Environments and Measures of these Environments. *Heredity*, 27: 15-23.

Fukuda, T., 1960. The Correlation Between the Mulberry Leaves taken by the Silkworm, the Silk Protein in the Silk Gland and Silk Filament, *Bull Seric. Exp. Stn.* 15(10): 605-610.

Fukuda, T., Kameyama, T. and M. Matsuda., 1963. A Correlation Between the Mulberry Leaves Consumed by the Larvae in Different Ages of the Larval Growth and Production of Cocoon Fibre by the Silkworm Larva and of the Eggs Laid by the Silkworm Moth. *Bull. Seric. Exp. Stn.* 18(3): 165-171.

Game, T., 1976. Recent Concepts and Trends in Silkworm Breeding. *Farming Japan*. 10(6): 11-12.

Gamo, T., 1983. Biochemical Genetics and its Application to the Breeding of the Silkworm. *JARQ*. 16(4): 264-272.

Gamo, T. and T. Hirabayashi, 1983. Genetic Analysis of Growth Rate, Pepation Rate and some Quantitative Characters by Diallel Analysis in the Silkworm, Japan. *J. Breed*. 33(2): 1 78-190.

Govindan, R., Magadum, B, Satenahalli, S.B., Suhas Yelshetty, V.B. Magadum and T.K. Narayanaswamy., 1990. Comparative Variability in Cocoon and Pupal Weights, Ovariole Length, Ovariole Egg Number and Fecundity in some Pure Breeds and Fl Hybrids of Silkworm, *Bombyx mori L*. Mysore J. Agri. Sci. 24: pp. 86-88.

Grekov, D. and N. Petkov, 1989. Breeding Genetic Evaluation of some White Cocoon Races of the Silkworm, *Bombyx mori*, II. Manifestation of Heterosis and Inheritance of Quantitative Traits. *Anim. Set*. 22 (6): 107.

Grifftag, B. and E. Zsloroa, 1971. Heterosis Associated with Genotype-environment Interactions. *Genetics*. 68: 443-445.

Harada, C.I 1949. On the Hybrid Effect of Economical Characters in the Silkworm. *J. Seric.Sd. Jpn*. 18.

Harada, C., 1952. On the Double Cross of the Silkworms. *Japan. J. Breed*. 2(2): 3.

Harada, C., 1954. On the Three Way Cross of the Silkworm *Japan, J. Breed*. 3(3 & 4): 99.

Harada, C., 1956. On the Relation Between Commercial Character and Their Fl Hybrids in *Bombyx mori*. *Proc. Int. Genet. Symp*. pp. 352-356.

Harada, C., 1961. On the Heterosis of Quantitative Characters in the Silkworm. *Bull Seric. Exp. Stn*. 1 7(1): 50-52.

Harada, C., Kimura. K, and Aoki, H., 1961. On the Effect of Hybrid Vigour on the Quantitative Characters Concerned with Reeling of Cocoons. *Acta Sericologia*, 37: 42-45.

Hassanien, H. and M. F. E. Sharawwy, 1960. Biological Studies on Certain Races of Silkworm *Bombyx mori L. J. Silkworm* IB(12): 376-390.

Hassaneln and M.F.E. Sharawwy., 1962. The Effect of Feeding the Silkworms, Bombyx Mori with Different Varieties on the Fecundity of Moths. *J. Silkworm*. 14: 163-170.

Hiratsuka, E., 1969. Historical Review of the Silkworm Varieties in Japan. *Sanshika Gaku Kenkyusho*, Tokyo.

Hirobe, T., 1956. An Analysis of Heterosis Made with the Silkworm. Proc. Int. Genet Symp, Tokyo Sci. Council of Jpn. 357-361

Hirobe, T., 1985. On the Recent Advancement of Silkworm Breeding in Japan. Tamagawa Univ. 2-17-19, Gakuen-cho, *Highshikurume-Shi Jpn*, 157-167.

Hirobe, T. and H. Ohl, 1954. On the Studies of Heterosis in *Bombyx mori L*, Japan. *J. Breed*. 4: 1.

Jaroonchi, J., 1972. Batch Selection of Thai Polyvoltine Silkworm Races15K and 15KY. *Bull TJ. Seric. Res. Train*. Cent. 2: 56-58.

Jolly, M. S., 1983. Silkworm Breeding in India. In. Silkworm *Genetics and Breeding*. Nait Semin. Silk Res. Devt. Bangalore, India, 1-9.

Kadkol, G.P.O., I.J. Anand and R.P. Sharma, 1984. Combining Ability and Heterosis in Sunflower. *Ind. J. Genet*. 44(3) 447-451.

Kalpana, G.V., 1992. Breeding of Superior Races of Silkworm *Bombyx mori. L* for Tropical Climates. Ph.D., Thesis, Univ. of Mysore, Mysore.

Kantaratnakul, Jharvoraanukulklt, C., Wongthong, S., Chareonying, S., Camplranon, A., and P. Saksoong., 1987 Diallei Crosses with Polyvoltine Strains of Thai Silkworm *Bombyx mori L.* XV Int. Seric. Cong. *Sericologia*, 27 (2): 279-286.

Kasivishwanathan, K., M.N.S. Lyengar and S. Krifthnawami, 1970. Effect of Feeding Leaves Grown Under Different Systems of Mulberry Cultivation on the Silkworm Cocoon Crops. *Ind. J. Seric.* 9(1): 53-58.

Kasturi Bai, A.R., 1983. Silkworm Rearing, Pests and Diseases Nat. Sem. on Silk Res. and Dev. Bangalore, 1-16.

Katsumata, K., 1948. On the Study of Hybrid Vigour in the Silkworm. Fuji-San 1.

Kaushik, L.S., D.P. Sing and R. S. Paroda., 1984. Line x Tester Analysis for Fixed Effect Model in Cotton (*Gossipium hirsutum L.*) *Theor. Appl Genet.* 68: 487-491.

Kempthorne, O., 1957. *An Introduction to Genetics Statistics*. John Wiley and Sons, New York, p. 631.

Kobayashi, E., T. Qamo and Y. Ohtsnka., 1968. Analysis of Heterosis by Means of Diallel Cross Between Different Regional Varieties of the Silkworm 1. Data of a pilot Experiment. *J. Seric. Sd. Jpn.* 37(2): 144-150.

Kobayashi, J., Edinuma, H.E. and M. Kobayashi., 1986. Effet of Temperature on the Diapause Egg Production in the Tropical Race of the Silkworm *Bombyx mori J. Seric. Sci. Japan* 55 (4): 343-348.

Kogure, K., 1932. The Influence of Light and Temperature on Certain Characters of Silkworm, *Bombyx mori. J.* Dept. Agri. Kyushu Imperial Univ. 4: 1-93.

Kovalov, D.A., 1970. *Silkworm Breeding Techniques*. Central Silk Board, Bombay, India.

Krishnaswami, S., 1978. New Technology of Silkworm Rearing. CSR & T Bulletin No. 2, Central Silk Board, Bangalore, India, 1-23.

Krishnaswami, S., M.S. Jolly and G. Subba Rao., 1964. Diallel Analysis of Quantitative Characters in Multivoltine Races of Silkworm. *Ind. J. Genet & PI. Breed*. 24: 213-222.

Krishnaswami, S., Noamani, K.R. and M. Ahsan., 1970a. Studies on the Quality of Mulberry Leaves and Silkworm Cocoon Crop Production I. Quality Differences Due to Variaties *Ind. J. Seric*. 9(1): 1-10.

Krishnaswami, S., Ahsan, M. and T.P. Sriharan., 1970b. Studies on the Quality of Mulbery Leaves and Silkworm Cocoon Crop Production I. Quality Differences Due to Leaf Maturity *Ind. J. Seric*. 9 (1): 11-25.

Krishnaswami, S., and B. L. Tikoo., 1971. A Comparative Study of Performance of Pure Races Currently under Rearing in Mysore State. *Ind. J. Seric*. 10(1); 66-71.

Krishnaswami, and M.N. Narasimhanna., 1974. Large Scale Trials on Blvoltinc Hybrids in Mysore State. *Ind. J. Genet. & P. Dreed*. 34A: 229-236.

Malik, M.A., 1992. Studies on the Performance and Adaptation of Bivoltine Races of Silkworm *Bombyx mori L* of Kashmir and Evaluation of Heterosis in Their Hybrids Under Temperate and Sub-tropical Elimates. Ph. D. Thesis Univ. of Mysore, Mysore.

Mariabashetty, V.G., 1991. Evolution of Superior Bivoltine Races of Silkworm *Bombyx mori L.* for Tropics Ph.D. Thesis, Univ. of Mysore, Mysore.

Matsumura, S. and Y. Takeuchi, 1950. Experiments on the Nutrition of Silkworm I. The Nutrition of Modern Hybrid Races. *J. Sen. Sci. Jpn.* 19: 192-200.

Morohoshi, S., 1969. The Control of Growth and Development in *Bombyx mori*. Relationship Between Environmental Moulting and Voltine Characters. *Proc. Jpn. Acad.* 45: 797-802.

Muslim, N.M., 1986. Trails on Multiple Silkworm Rearing in Spring-post Spring Seasons in Pakistan, *Pak. J. For.* 36 (I): 53-58.

Nacheva, I., 1980. Heterosis Effect on some Technological Qualities of Cocoons and Silk Fibres in the Silkworm *Bombyx mori*. *Zhivotnov'D Nauki*, 17: 88-94.

Nacheva and Znnka, 1989. Phenotypic and Genotypic Characterisation of Silkworm Character during the Different Seasons of Silkworm Feeding. *Genet. Sel* 22 (3): 242-247.

Nanavathy., 1965. *Silk from Grub to Glamour*. Central Silk Board, Bombay, India.

Nanjundaswamy, L., 1997. Studies on the Combining Ability in Silkworm Bombyx mori L. Ph.D Thesis, University of Mysore, Mysore.

Narasimhanna, M.N. 1976. Contributions to the Genetics of Silkworm. Ph.D. Thesis, University of Mysore, Mysore.

Narashimhanna, M.N. and S. Krishnaswami, 1972. Improved Techniques of Silkworm Rearing. Seminar on Sericulture Organised by CSR & TI, Mysore. pp. 1-11.

Narashimhanna, M.N., Chandrashekaralah, R.G. Geethadevi, N. Muneera and G. Prabha, 1976. Ecogenetic Attributes of the Newly Evolved Bivoltine Hybrid "Nandi" in *Bombyx mori L. Proc. Dunn. Dobzhansky Syrup*. Genet. 379-386.

Narasimhanna, M.N. and M.R. Rajashekarashetty., 1979, Line × Tester Analysis of *Bombyx mori L.* Isolation of Multivoltine Hybrids for Karnataka State E.S.A.P. Bangalore.

Narayanan, E. S.L. S. Prahlada Rao and H. A. Nagaraja Rao, 1964. Studies on Correlation Between the duration of Mating and Number of Viable Eggs Laid by the Silk Moth, *Bombyx mori L.* I. Effect of Duration of Copulation of the Resulting Number of Viable Eggs. *Ind. J. Seric.* 3(2): 1-9.

Narayanan, E.S., L.S. Prahlada Rao and C.V. Venkataramu., 1967. Effect of Varietal Feeding, Irrigation Levels and Nitrogen Fertilization on the Larval Development and Cocoon Characters of *Bombyx mori L. Ind. J. Seric.* 1(2): 1-5.

Nirmal Kumar, S., 1995. Studies on the Synthesis of Appropriate Silkworm Breeds (*Bombyx mori L.*) for Tropics. Ph. D. Thesis, Univ. of Mysore, Mysore.

Orozco, F., 1976. Heterosis and Genotype Environment Interaction: Theoritical and Experimental Aspects. Bulletin Technique, Deptt. de Genetique Animal. Institute National de la RacJ-ierche Agronomique No. 24; 43-52.

Osawa, K., 1936. History of Silkworm Varieties. History of Silk Industry in Japan, Dainiton Sanshikai, Tokyo.

Osawa, K. and C. Harada, 1944. Studies on the Fl Hybrids of the Silkworm III. On the Effect of Heterosis. *Bull Seric. Expt. Stn. Jpn.* 12: 183-211.

Pai, I.K., 1988. Studies on the Genetic Effects of Chemical Growth Regulators and Their Utility in the Improvement of Races of Silkworm, *Bombyx mori*. Ph. D. Thesis, Univ. of Mysore, Mysore.

Perkins, J.M. and J.L. Jinks., 1968. Environmental and Genotype Environmental Components of Variability III. Multiple Lines and Crosses. *Heredity*. 23: 339-356.

Pershad, G. D., Datta, R. K., Bhargava, S.K., H.V. Vijaya Kumar and M.S. Jolly, 1986. Combining Ability Analysis in Multivoltine Races of *Bombyx mori L. Sericologia*. 26: 307-315.

Petkov, N., 1975. Investigation on Combining Ability of Some Inbred Lines of *Bombyx mori. Genet. Sel.* 8(2): 128-136.

Petkov, N., Georgi, A., Mladenov and J. Nacheva, 1979. Effect of Mating Length of Silk Moths of some Inbred Silkworm *Bombyx mori* Lines on Silkworm Seed Quantity and Quality. *Zhivotnov'D Nauki* 16 (3): 116-122.

Petkov, N and A. Yolov, 1980. Influence of Cocoon Size and Weight on Heterosis Effect in Silkworm *Bombyx mori L. Genet. Sel Bulg*. 12(4): 286-291.

Petkov, N., Nacheva, Y., A. Yolov and O. Mladenov., 1982 Apprasing the Combinative Ability of Some Silkworm Lines. *Animal Science*. 19(2), p. 121.

Rajanna, G. S., 1989. Evolution of Suitable Bivoltine Races of Silkworm *Bobmyx mori L.* for Tropics. Ph.D. Thesis, University of Mysore, Mysore.

Raje Urs, S., 1988. Studies on the Genetics of Heterosis and Voltinism in Silkworm *Bombyx mori L.* Ph.D. Thesis, University of Mysore, Mysore.

Raju, P.J., 1990. Studies on the Hybridization and Synthesis of New Breeds of Silkworm *Bombyx mori L.* Ph.D. Thesis, University of Mysore, Mysore.

Raman, S.M and Ahmed, S.U., 1988. Stability Analysis for Silk Yield in some Promising Genotypes of Silkworm *Bombyx mori L.* In: *Proc. Int Cong. Trop. Seric. Prac.* pp: 27-30.

Rana, B.S. and B. R. Murthy, 1971. Genetic Analysis of Resistance to Stem Borer in sorghum. *Ind. J. Genet. & pl Breed*. 28(3): 231-238.

Rao, N.G.P., Rana, V. K. S. and D.P. Tripathi, 1968. Linex Tester Analysis of Combining Ability in Sorghum. Ind. *J. Genet & pl. Breed*. 26(3): 231-238.

Rayar, S.G. and R. Govindan., 1990. Performance of some Single and Three-way Cross Hybrids in Silkworm *Bombyx mori L* for Larval Traits. *Entomon*, 15(3 8s 4): 183-186.

Sammuel, C.J.A., Hill, J. Breese, C.L. and Davies, A., 1970. Assessing and Predicting Environmental Response in *Lolium perenne J. Agric. Sci. Camb*., 75: 1-9.

Satenahalli, S. B., G. Govindan and J. V. Goad., 1989. Heterosis Studies for some Quantitative Traits in Silkworm. *Bombyx mori*. *Ind. J. Seric*. 28(1): 100-102.

Satenahalli, S. B.V.R. Govindan and J. V. Goud., 1990. Analysis of Heterosis for some Quantitative Traits in Silkworm *Bombyx mori L*. Mysore. *J. Agri. Sci*. 24: 214-221.

Sengupta, K., 1969. An Analysis of Genotype—Environment Interaction in some Races of Silkworm *Bombyx mori L. Ind. J. Seric*. 8 (J): 4-6.

Sengupta, K., Yusuf, M. R. and S.P. Grover., 1974. Hybrid Vigour and Genetic Analysis of Quantitative Traits in Silkworm. *Ind. J. Genet*. 34(A): 240-256.

Sengupta, K., 1988. Bivoline Rasing in the Plains and Plateaus of South India. Indian Silk, 27 (7): 25-27.

Setty, K.L.T. and B. Singh, 1977. Line x Tester Analysis of Combining Ability in Sunflower. Panth NagarJ. of Res. 25(2): 23-26.

Sldhu, N.S., S. Venugopala Filial, Kamala Singh and R. Sreenivasan, 1968. The Performance of an Evolved Multivoltine Silkworm *Breed. Ind. J. Seric*. VH(1): 6-12.

Sidhu, N.S., Tikoo, B. L., Kamala Singh and S. Venngopal Pillai, 1969. New Hybrid of Silkworm for Commercial Crops for Multivoltine Regions. *Silkworm Inf. Bull* 1(2): 18-25.

Singh, C. and T. Hirobe, 1964. Studies on the Hybrid Vigour of Back-crosses in the Silkworm: With Special Reference to the Crosses (Tropical x Japanese) Under Different Rearing Temperature. Bull. Fac. Agri. Tamagava University 12: 43-53.

Singh, T.H., S. P. Gupta and P.S. Phul, 1971. Line x Tester Analysis of Combining Ability in Cotton. *Ind. J. Genet. & pi Breed.* 31. No. 2: 316-321.

Sprague, G.F. and L.A. Tatum, 1942. General Vs. Specific Combining Ability in Single Crosses of Corn. *J. Amer. Soc*. Aaron. 34: 923-932

Sreerama Reddy, G. Krishnamurthy, N.B, and G. Subramanya, 1986. Analysis of Heterosis and Superdominance in the Fi Hybrids of Newly Evolved Polyvoltine Races (MW_1 and MW_{303}) x Popular Bivoltine Races (NB_7, NB_{18}, NB_4D_2 AND KA) of Silkworm *Bomyx mori L. Nat. Sem. Prob. Prosp. Seric. India. Vellore, Tamil Nadu, Abstract No. 32.*

Strickberger, M.W., 1976. *Environmental Genetics and Gene Expression*. Genetics. 2nd Edition, pp. 182-201.

Strunnikov, V. A., 1971. Production of Silkworm Hybrids Differentiating into White Female and Dark Male Eggs. *Dok. Akad. Nauk*. USSR. 201, 5.

Subba Rao, G., 1983. Line x Tester analysis of some Character in Bivoltine Silkworms. *Abst. Nat. Sem. Silk Res. and Development*. Bangalore, p. 15.

Subba Rao, G* and V. Sahal., 1989. Combining Ability and Heterosis Studies in Bivoltine Strains of Silkworms *Bombyx mori L*. Uttar Pradesh. *J. Zoology* 9(12): ISO-164.

Subramanya, G., 1985. Ecogenetic Approach for Determination of High Yielding Breeds of Silkworm *Bombyx mori L.* Ph.D. Thesis, University of Mysore, Mysore.

Suzuki, C., 1954. Microclimate in some Simple Rearing Rooms for the Early Stage of the Silkworm. *Bull Seric. Exp. Stn.* 14: 343-350.

Takasaki, T., 1968. Utilization of Heterosis in Silkworm Breeding, Recent Advances in Breeding. *Jap. Soc. Breed.* 9: 47-55.

Tayade, D.S., 1987. Heterosis Effect on the Economic traits of New Hybrids of Silkworm *Bombyx mori L* under Marathwada Conditions. *Proc. Nal Sem. Prospects Prob. Seric. inlnd. Vellore.* pp. 168-174.

Tazima, Y., 1962. Silkworm Egg: Scientific Brochure-1 Central Silk Board, Bombay, India, 1-49.

Tikoo, B. L. Kaplla, M. L. and S. Krishnaswam, L, 1971. Large Scale Trails on the Comparative Performance of Multivoltine x Bivoltine Hybrids of Mulberry Silkworms in Mysore State. *Ind. J. Seric.* 10(1): 57-65.

Toyama, K., 1905. Sericulture in Siam. Dainihon Sansrd Keinko. 24-26.

Toyama, K., 1906 a. Mendel's Law of Heridity as Applied to the Silkworm Crosses. *Biol Zentrulbl*, 26: 321-334.

Toyama, K., 1906b. Breeding Methods of Silkworm. *Sangyo Shimpo*. 158: 282-286.

Udupa, S. and V. Gowda., 1988. Heterosis Expression in Silk Productivity of Different Crosses of Silkworm, *Bombyx mori Sericologia*, 28(3): 395-399.

Ueda, S., R. Kimura and K. Suruki, 1969. Studies on the Growth of the Silkworm *Bombyx mori*. II. The Influence of Rearing Condition upon the Larval

Growth, Productivity of Silk Substance and Eggs and Boil off Loss in Cocoon Shell. *Bull. Seric. Expt. Stn.* 23: 290-293.

Ueda, S., R. Kimura and K. Suzuki, 1971. Studies on the Growth of the Silkworms *Bombyx mori*. III. Relative Increase in Body Weight and Silk Gland Weight in the 5th instar larvae *Bull. Seric, Expt*. Stn. 25: 20.

Ueda, S., R. Kimura and K. Suzuki., 1975. Studies on the Growth of the Silkworm *Bombyx mori*. IV Mutual Relationship Between the Growth in the Fifth instar Larvae and Productivity of Silk Substance and Eggs. *Bull Seric Expt*. Sin. 26(3): 233-247.

Veeraiah, T.M. 1999. Studies on the Exploitation of Heterosis in Silkworm *Bombyx mori. L* Ph.D Thesis, University of Mysore, Mysore.

Vijaya Raghavan, K. and P.K. Das., 1992. Studies on Heterosis and Combining Ability in some Multivoltine and Bivoltine Breeds of the Silkworm *Bombyx mori L. Ind. J. Seric*. 31(1) 77-80.

Watanabe, K., 1918. Studies on the Voltinism in the Silkworm Bombyx mori I. Inheritance of Bivoltine v/s Quadra Voltines. *Bull. Seric. Expt Stn. Japan*, 3: 439-456.

Watanabe, K., 1919. Studies on the Voltinism in Silkworm *Bombyx mori L* Inheritance of Voltinism v/s Multivoltine *Bull Seric. Expt. Stn Japan*, 4: 87-106.

Watanabe, H., 1961. Manifestation of Heterosis on Egg Laying Abiligy in the Silkworm *Bombyx mori L.J. Seric. Expt. Stn. Jpn*. 30: 345-350.

Watanabe, H., 1961. Studies on Difference in the Variability of Larval Body and Cocoon Weights Between Single Cross and Three - Way Cross or Double Cross Hybrids in the Silk Worm, *Bombyx mori. J. Sen'c. Sci. Jpn*, 30: 463-467.

White, T.G. and T.R. Richmond., 1963. Heterosis and Combinating Ability in Top and Diallel Crosses Among Primitive, Foreign and Cultivated American Upland Cottons. *Crop. Set.* 3: 58-62.

Yokoyama, T., 1957. On the Application of Heterosis in Japanese Sericulture Proc. *Int. Symp. Suppl.* Vol. *Cytologia*, pp. 527-537.

Yokoyama, T., 1962. Synthesized Science of Sericulture. Central Silk Board, India. p. 283.

Yokoyama, T., 1963. Sericulture. Ann. Rev, *Entomol.* Vol. 8, Ann. rev. Inc. California, pp. 287-306.

Yokoyama, T., 1973. Studies on the Improvement in the Efficiency of Egg Production by means of Polyhybrids. *Reports of Silk Science Res.* Inst 22: 6-24.

Yokoyama, T., 1974. Utilization of Heterosis in Japanese Seirculture. *Ind. J Genet. & PL Breed.* 34A: 206-210.

Yokoyama, T., 1979. Silkworm Selection and Hybridization. In: *Genetics in Relation to Insect Management.* Working Papers. The Rockfeller Foundation, 71-83.

INDEX